"When it comes to stand-up, online dating, and comedic writing, Traci Kanaan has a nice rack."

—ROBERT ITSCHNER, JR.
Facebook friend

"Traci went on these dates so you wouldn't have to!"

—JOHN D. HOOPER
Improvisational comedy performer and Comedy Fan

"A unique mash-up of sassy and sensitive, shyly transparent yet achingly acerbic, with a heart as big as... well, as big as those beautiful things she covers it with... "

—GEORG WILLIAM
went on a few dates with Traci

"Traci is the Queen of the blow-off... all without touching anyone! Funny answers to guys with no sense, or sense of humor. Online banter you wish you'd said."

—MARK BYRNE
The Balloon Guy
entertainer and colleague of Traci

"Some years ago, Traci Kanaan introduced herself to me, saying, 'I get on stage, play piano, and tell dick jokes.' That should tell you all you need to know about her viciously funny worldview. And this book, detailing her withering ripostes to online suitors, is a devastating peek into how a smart, confident woman looks for love—or something like it—while refusing to give up the yardstick by which she measures the inferior species."

—David Abolafia
Writer, "Jeopardy!" champion, Scrabble lover,
Mr. December 2009 "Real Men Wear Pink"
60-Mile Men calendar for the Susan G. Komen Foundation

"Traci's comedy has always been hilariously stranger than fiction. It's reassuring to see that her love life is no different."

—Keith Kong
Mentalist, colleague of Traci

"She is amazing, but I don't kiss and tell. My wife might kill me. Okay, I'm not married at the present time because I did kiss and tell."

—Al Woods
Owner of The Social Club (TSC) in Nashville, TN,
and Traci's friend

"Online dating has never been so sassy! This book is a must have for anyone who has ever swiped right!"

—Michael Richards
met Traci at a hypnosis conference in 2016

"There's not enough good things to say about Traci— as a friend, as a client, as someone who is a fantastic entertainer—she's magnificent! Her stories of online dating are enough to keep you engaged and laughing all the way to the altar. Curl up with a beverage… and a napkin so you don't spit your drink out laughing."

—MICHELLE MOSHER REBAHN
Comedy Fan & Traci's insurance agent

"As a Comedy Booker and longtime friend, I can tell you that this beautiful and wonderful woman is not only Hilarious but a multi-talented Musical Genius, as well. SHOCKING that she is still single… Until you read her responses to her potential dates."

—LARRY SILVER
Groucho Productions

"Traci was so funny I shit my pants. I mean, I pee'd my pants. Either way, bring extra pants."

—BOB HANNAFORD
*French Connection Events Owner, New Orleans, LA
and has booked Traci for several of his events*

"When I saw Traci's picture, I couldn't understand why she'd need online dating. When I read some of the responses she got, and her replies, I laughed, but also felt ashamed to be a man. Then I looked at her picture again and got over it."

—MIKE BRENNAN
Writer, divorced dad and Facebook friend

"Traci takes on dating 'tongue in cheek' – to keep other tongues outta her throat! She'll have you rolling in the aisles and thanking your husband that you're off the 'meet market' with the hilarious hijinks she endures all in the name of love – or at least dinner and a decent O!"

—TIFFANY MARIE MCANALLY
Comedy Fan, and yes, that's her real name

"I went on a date with Traci and the entire time I was afraid I would end up in her act... (I'm not in this book, am I? *Am I, Traci?*)"

—ERIC BOHNER
went on a date with Traci, and yes, that's his real name

"I would rather take a punch to the nut sack than be on the receiving end of her sarcasm and wit."

—CASEY KENSINGER
coincidentally, the undertaker
for both of Traci's parents

"Hey!"

...and other
scintillating
mating calls from the
online dating world

Traci Kanaan

Year of the Book
135 Glen Avenue
Glen Rock, PA 17327

ISBN 13: 978-1-945670-62-6
ISBN 10: 1-945670-62-2

The methods described within this book are the author's personal thoughts. They are not intended to be a definitive set of instructions for this project. You may discover there are other methods and materials to accomplish the same end result. (Like anyone would want this result.)

To protect the privacy of certain individuals the names and identifying details have been changed... but if it sounds like you, it probably is.

ACKNOWLEDGMENTS

I'd like to thank the following people for making this book possible:

My parents.
Without them (and the bottle of Cold Duck they drank on New Year's Eve in 1968) I would not be. You gave me life, a sense of humor, and an amazing set of tits that has taken me to places I never imagined I'd go. You encouraged me to find the light in the darkest moments. From there, I discovered just how strong I was when I thought I was most broken. And through all of it... I still have an amazing set of tits.

Everyone who had something to do with creating an online dating website.
Without you... this book would not be. Thank you for creating the online platforms which have the potential for millions of people to meet their happily ever after... or at least their unhappily ever after.

Everyone on the online dating websites who wrote me.
Without you... this book would not be either. I know most of you had no idea whatever you wrote me was going to end up in a book, but in my defense, I really didn't know I was going to write this book until after you wrote me so much stupid shit.

Everyone I met online who later met me for coffee or took me out on a date.
I hope our date was a positive experience and it made your life better in some small way.
Except for that one fucker who said I was fat.
Fuck you.

My Facebook Family.
Without you liking and sharing my crazy online dating posts... I never would have thought to write this book.

There are only good times... and better stories.
The choice is yours.

With love, Traci

INTRODUCTION

*"Do not judge my story by the chapter you
walked in on." ~Anonymous*

After 19 years of marriage, I found myself divorced
and living alone in my mid 40s. Rather than face the
possibility of living alone the rest of my life, I did
what millions of others have done and tried online
dating.

When I dated 25 years ago, my options included ads
in the Personals section in the backs of free
magazines, and Matchmaker, Inc. I did both of these
in 1991-1994.

In 1991, I was fresh out of college and my fellow
students with real majors had trouble finding work
during the recession... so me and my degree in
music were shit out of luck. After 9 months of
courtship, I had totally failed to hook up with my high
school sweetheart and prom date, probably because
he was gay. I had also failed to find a husband in 4
years at my college where the girl/guy ratio was 5:1,
and that didn't account for numerous theater and
music majors who were gay too. I ended up back
home working at the local clock store, living with my

parents, only to find all of my friends had gotten married, gotten jobs, and moved on. Tired of spending my nights at home by myself after helping married men choose gifts for their wives all day at the clock store, I placed an ad in the local *Scene* magazine in Cleveland, OH... and received numerous responses within days.

Some of them were great. Others... not so much. One of them I dated for a few months. He was a salesman for a cosmetics company, so my perks in addition to an occasional dinner out, were free coconut-scented shampoos and conditioners. He was gorgeous, but quirky with what I now recognize as "extreme behaviors." He carried my high school senior photo with him wherever he went, and showed me off to everyone. I'd never had anyone do that with me before. He kept saying, "My high school never had pretty girls like you." I was so flattered, until he showed me his yearbook, and I realized he went to an all-male Catholic school.

He had fantasies about being a police officer, and often played with handcuffs while we were watching cop shows on TV. One time he handcuffed me to the bed and licked my toes until I screamed. It was exciting... and scary all at once. At 22, it didn't occur to me I could be dating a real whack job. At 42, it did occur to me how much I liked my toes getting licked at 22. But that's another story. Thankfully, he came over for dinner at my parent's house one time, and rather than chime in to the existing dinner conversation which didn't interest him, he read the newspaper... at the dinner table. My parents were pissed, and suggested I break up with him, which I did.

He pleaded to get back together with me a few weeks later. We met for lunch to discuss it, and I remember he looked horrible. He admitted he had lost 15 pounds in two weeks. He had begun replacing all his meals with vitamins, because "vitamins have all the nutritional value I need to live." I listened to my instincts, and the relationship was permanently severed, and I went on to date many others who never worked out either.

A year later, I joined Matchmakers, International. I didn't know how badly they needed women, and paid $1500 for my first 8 matches, which lasted a month. They asked me to re-join, unlimited matches for $200, so I did. They sent me so many matches, I could barely keep up! I was taking note cards on dates, because I couldn't keep them all straight.

At one point, I was dating two guys named Jeff, who drove Mustang convertibles, that were engineers for

Ford, and had just gotten their own apartment. I was a prime catch then... 22 years old, with a college degree, never married and no children that I knew of. Matchmakers was pairing me with doctors, attorneys, engineers, CEOs of companies... all who could afford the $1500 price tag much more than I could... but none of them stuck.

My friends loved the stories about my numerous dates, but members of my family were horrified I did not meet someone through the traditional methods: being set up on dates by other family members. Well connected as they were in the community, my family didn't know anyone my age. My extended family lived 80 miles away in Youngstown, OH, which was not known for its formidable dating pool of eligible bachelors. My parents wrote me off as desperate. I began dating the eligible men that came into the clock shop... both UPS drivers. I was lonely, did not want to remain so, and at the "way past my prime" age of 25, I was the "Old Maid" of the Italian side of the family as both of my older cousins had found their husbands by the age of 15.

I ended up meeting the man who would eventually become my husband of 19 years via an AOL.com search, and we met in person at a service club convention in Toronto, Canada. I followed him to

Florida, where we had many happy years together, but sometimes good things come to an end. I felt I became a better person during the 19 years we were together, but "statistics" will call our marriage "a total failure." Of course, for any marriage to be considered "successful," one or both spouses have to *DIE*. Just to put how stupid this is into perspective... the only other people who think Death = Success are funeral directors, pest control companies, and terrorists.

Fast forward 20+ years. It was January 2015, and I separated from my husband at the age of 45. I peeked into the world of online dating, and was overwhelmed at the choices! PlentyOfFish.com, OKCupid.com, Match.com, AdultFriendFinder.com, eHarmony.com, and Craigslist.org, as well as several smart phone apps to choose from including Zoosk, Bumble, and Tinder.

I was on the world wide web, with thousands of people *oogling* my profile and pictures. In some respects with online dating, you've been spared the awkwardness of having to dress up and hit the smoky bar scene, only to make eye contact with a random stranger who is a) married, b) stupid, c) more interested in your friend, or d) all of the above.

You can now spend your time reading hundreds of profiles from the comfort of your home, and all you have to do is hope they're real and not a) married, b) stupid, c) more interested in anyone else, or d) all of the above. Someone can simply SEE you're online, and they send you a quick email or an instant chat message. Sometimes the guy you're talking to is the guy pictured. Sometimes he isn't. You have no idea until you're at a coffee house waiting for your man to show up. *If* he shows up.

So I put up my profile online, trying to make it as accurate as possible, and soon discovered I was the only one in the entire universe who wasn't afraid to be authentic. I often wondered how someone got to be 53 years old and couldn't find any words to describe who he was. Under "description" he would write, "I hate describing myself," "ask me anything," or "smell ya later."

The dating "inquiries" you're about to read were received during a 3-year period while I was simultaneously divorcing my husband *and* taking care of my mother who had rampant diabetes and dementia.

My being separated and in the midst of a divorce didn't bother most men. (Ironically, a man in the midst of a separation or divorce seems to bother most women.) Most men thought I was being a "good daughter" for taking care of my mother... right up until I had to cancel a date because my mother was setting up her own "blind dates" with every EMT in the county via medical emergency.

And then... I'm a nationally touring stand-up comedian, which most guys think is cool as Hell. But just when I thought I had found "Mr. Good Enough To Date For A Few Months" I was out the door for a multi-week comedy tour or even worse – headed to perform on a week-long swinger's cruise, as much of my comedy work centers around "sexually adventurous adults." I can re-assure you, there is no second date in my future when the next words I hear are: "You're performing on a *WHAT?*"

Between the stresses of my divorce and caring for my mother, I couldn't get on the road and perform as much as I was accustomed. In order to keep my sanity and my comedy brain working, I began writing responses to the dumber emails I received, and posting them on Facebook for my friends and comedy fans to read. Pretty soon I found my "Online Dating" posts were very popular and frequently shared. Several people said, "You should write a book."

TA DA!!!

So... here we are. This book is primarily a collection of first emails I received from men via online dating, coupled with "my responses." Before you read the emails I received, I'd like you, the reader, to know that this book is NOT written from the perspective that "I am a perfect Goddess" and "all men are stupid." "My responses" are often things I would have *liked* to have written back, but chose not to because some of them are snarky and downright bitchy, and overall I'm really a nice "live and let live" kind of lady. Some of the responses I really did send, because the dickhead who wrote me first had it coming. I'll let you decide which ones are "witch."

It's important to note when you read this book, I am not bashing men. I LOVE MEN! All men are not stupid. Stupidity is not gender specific! Don't get your MAN-ties in a wad over this. If I am making fun of anything, I am making light of the fact that men (and women) have no fucking idea how to sell themselves to another human being, which is the ultimate bottom line of online dating. No man or woman needs to apologize for their gender, race, or anything else.

Warning! There are numerous typos in this book. I made an editorial decision to copy and paste the emails I received without corrections, as I felt they best conveyed the intent and personality of the senders. This book also contains strong language. (In all fairness, conversations you have with me will likely contain strong language, too.) Sometimes, "gosh," "golly," and "shucks" just don't convey the fucking frustration I feel. Apologies in advance on both accounts, but it was more important to me that everything in this book be "authentic" and not some politically correct cover-up of less fortunate "English impaired" individuals.

Also included in this book, are some of my online dating stories, fun facts and trivia about online dating, and 40 things you should never say on a first date. I ended up saying most of them because I'm a comedian and I can't help myself.

This just so happens to be a humorous book about online dating, that just so happens to be written by a comedian who just so happens to be a female. Many of the emails I received could've been written by the opposite sex just as easily. Everyone who has an online dating profile is hoping to find long lasting... err... short lasting... err... anything that remotely resembles the ideal of "love." "We" as human beings, just haven't thought about the best way to go about getting "love" all the way through sometimes.

Everything you're about to read is my perspective of the online dating experience, of my trying to find the timeless ideal of "love" through a bitmapped, digital filter. If you're in a relationship and you're happy, count your sweet blessings. If you're in a relationship and you're not happy, here is what you have to look forward to should you make a change.

If you're single... you know this Hell all too well. Pour yourself a glass of wine, sit back, and laugh with me.

ONLINE DATING PROFILE

In order to date online, you need an online dating profile. Mine evolved over the years, and certain websites asked for some details that others did not. The following is a summarization of all my dating profiles. I've had several of my friends read this, and they have verified the description of myself is accurate. If you're familiar with online dating, you'll notice my profile is more detailed and specific than other profiles. I'm not trying to attract just anyone. My goal is to attract men who are literate, educated, and have a sense of humor. I feel if someone is willing to read all the crazy stuff I wrote, chances are they are really looking for a stronger connection than just a booty call. By the time you read this... you should have a pretty good idea about who I am, and what I'm looking for.

Tagline: High Class, Low Maintenance

City: St Petersburg, Florida

Details: 47-year-old female, 5' 4" (163cm)

Religion: Non-religious

Ethnicity: Caucasian

Zodiac: Libra

Intent: Wants to date but nothing serious

Education: Bachelor's Degree

Personality: Free Thinker

Description:

I live in St Petersburg, FL. If you see my profile and live somewhere else, I'm traveling for work.

If you have a twisted sense of humor, like to laugh, and enjoy a woman who is comfortable in her skin... keep reading! You might be my kind of guy. If you take yourself seriously, take life seriously, aren't comfortable in your skin or can't read – stop reading! I am not for you.

My friends will tell you I'm a warm, easy going, friendly, intelligent, irrepressible creative and one of the funniest, quick-witted women you'll meet. My "filter" does not work very well, although I can be honest and humorous simultaneously. I will likely surprise you by saying the things most people think but never say, as well as saying the things most people never think. I am an independent thinker, strong in my convictions, and a very creative, free spirit. Myers Briggs: ENFP with ENTP hot flashes.

I travel a lot for work, and enjoy hitting places of interest using the Trip Advisor and Roadside America apps. Also I'm a big fan of art and cultural museums, tourist traps, nature walks, kayaking, exploring St. Petersburg and Tampa (or wherever I happen to be), and relaxing at clothing optional resorts. So long as it engages my mind and requires interaction with real human beings and my surroundings... I'm in!

What I'm Looking For

Positive, independent, intelligent, OPEN-minded, respectful, fun-loving people in St. Pete/Tampa, who have already found happiness within and want a quality woman to share adventures with. I love a "Carpe Diem/Seize The Day!" mindset. Bonus points if you have a flexible schedule and a valid passport. My work takes me to some very cool places, and I'd love a travel companion. Men without children or empty nesters only.

I'm allergic to smoke and bad breath, so you must be a non-smoker and drug free. Familiarity with "the lifestyle" and/or BDSM would be ideal, as a large part of my comedy and hypnosis work revolves around these markets.

What I'm Doing with My Life

I've been self-employed in some capacity for 20+ years. Currently, I'm a nationally touring musical comedian and stage hypnotist. WARNING: If you're easily offended – disregard this profile. If you can't possibly be offended – have a seat! First round is on you. ;)

In addition to being a comedian, I'm also a Certified Hypnotist and Certified Clinical Hypnotherapist, so I can help others get past issues that keep them from realizing their fullest potential. I also own and manage a rental property.

Family

No kids that I know of. Therapy human for 2 cats, Thelma & Louise.

Favorite Books & Authors:

Ayn Rand: *The Fountainhead, Atlas Shrugged*

Lewis Carroll: *Alice In Wonderland*

Marie Kondo: *The Life-Changing Magic of Tidying*

Foods:

Japanese/Sushi, Indian, Italian, Vietnamese, BBQ/Southern, Middle Eastern, and Thai.

OMG... Waffle House. There's nothing like being stacked, smothered, and covered!

I spend a lot of time thinking about...

everything, because there's potential for everything to be funny. It's an occupational hazard.

On a typical Friday night I am...

... either performing, out with friends, and often I'm lucky enough to do both.

You should message me if...

... you are a fun, intelligent, and positive person.

Thank you for taking the time to read my profile! ·

Now that you've read the profile, I hope you noticed that I intentionally wrote some things about myself that are not "mainstream" and might make some men a little uncomfortable, like being a hypnotist or that my comedy work revolves around "the lifestyle" and "BDSM." I do this for two reasons. First of all, it makes me stand out from the thousands of other profiles. Second, if these things about me make a guy uncomfortable, I'm perfectly fine with him rejecting me. I'd rather not waste my time meeting someone who already has negative opinions about these important aspects of my life. By writing these personal details, there is also a chance that a guy may read that and find hypnosis and/or the lifestyle intriguing… and THAT is precisely who I want to meet.

TIRE KICKERS

Here are some initial contact emails I received from "potential suitors," followed by my non-responses.

I don't typically respond to these emails, because they're what I call "tire kickers" and too lazy to read a profile. Many men and women aren't sure about online dating, so they get a free profile and start throwing out "feelers" to see if anyone is interested. They poke around the online dating community to see if something pokes back. They rarely bother to put any effort into describing themselves. Sometimes they're looking for their spouse or co-workers, and often times their profile is deleted within days or even minutes of being created, so you've wasted your time responding to The Invisible Man.

Perhaps I've missed meeting a lot of great guys simply because they didn't know what to say in an initial contact email. But I am a very social person, and don't want to be with someone who doesn't know what to say, or how to start a conversation.

Many of these emails I received more than once, from several different profiles. In every case, the guy completely failed to "sell himself" by distinguishing how he was different from the other millions of men out there. None of these guys took a sincere interest in the person they were writing to. None of these guys gave me a compelling reason to write them back. Welcome to the online dating equivalent of "robo calls."

HE: Hey

ME:

HE: Hi

ME:

HE: Hello

ME:

HE: hey there

ME:

HE: Heyyy what's up?

ME:

HE: hi ther

ME:

HE: hi there

ME:

HE: How are you doing?

ME:

HE: How's your day going?

ME:

HE: How are you this evening?

ME:

HE: Hey sexy

ME:

HE: Hey sexxy

ME:

HE: Hey sexxxy

ME:

HE: Hey sexy mama

ME:

HE: Nice tits

ME:

HE: Hey. How was it?!

ME:

HE: Hi good morning

ME:

HE: how are you sunshine

ME:

HE: I'd love to know you

ME:

HE: Wows

ME:

HE: He sexy how are you

ME:

HE: you are exquisite

ME:

HE: Hey Hottie

ME:

HE: Heyyyyy you :)

ME:

HE: Wanna chat?

ME:

HE: Take a chance you won't be sorry

ME:

HE: Hi! You're super pretty

ME:

HE: Hi no way you are 46

ME:

HE: You seem a little bit of a naughty minx

ME:

HE: Hey beautiful how are you doing today

ME:

HE: Love that smile.

ME:

HE: How was your week?

ME:

HE: Hi how are you doing tonight

ME:

HE: Hey how's your Friday?

ME:

HE: Hello sexy lady my name is _____. Let's get together

ME:

HE: hello there how are you doing?

ME:

HE: Hi how are you doing

ME:

HE: I have to say that your really sexy

ME:

HE: Definitely caught my attention beautiful eyes

ME:

HE: hello, how are you?

ME:

HE: Hey sexy wanna chat do you have kik

ME:

HE: If I may say so you are absolutely beautiful

ME:

HE: Hello. Hope you are doing well.

ME:

HE: You have incredible eyes.

ME:

HE: Cool tatoo

ME:

HE: Love the tat and those eyes

ME:

HE: Cool Tat!! So what are you up to today?

ME:

HE: hi wanna chat

ME:

HE: Hi there. I like what I see on your page.

ME:

HE: Would you like to hangout?

ME:

HE: can I ask you a question

ME:

HE: I was wondering if I could ask you a question

ME:

HE: hi cutie how are you would love to meet

ME:

HE: Hi there! I was trying to think of an amazing message that would separate me from all the others on here! However, I just want to ask if you might like to talk sometime? Lol

ME:

HE: Hello! You like long thick cocks

ME:

DUMB QUESTIONS

A wise man can learn more from a foolish question,
than a fool can learn from a wise answer.

Why do birds suddenly appear – every time – you are near? How many licks does it take to get to the center of a Tootsie Pop? Sweet dreams are made of this – who has a mind to disagree? What is the meaning of life? Why do people start emails with questions? Why don't people read my profile? What constitutes a dumb question? Why did I put so many questions in my opening paragraph of Dumb Questions? Exactly. Read on.

HE: Sex?

ME: I'm female. Duh.

- -

HE: Are you Italian?

ME: No. Swedish and Korean.

- -

HE: What's shaken?

ME: A martini.

HE: Do you string your string cheese or bite it?

ME: Neither. I wait for real cheese.

HE: Do you know Rami Salami?

ME: Yes. He's Oscar Meyer's porkier cousin.

HE: Have you ever walked on hot coals doing a fire walk?

ME: Yes, I was married for 19 years.

(My profile name on one site is based on a quote from The Mad Hatter from *Alice In Wonderland*, which is where I believe this question came from.)

HE: Do you know why the mad hatter was mad?

ME: Because she spent countless hours writing the perfect online dating profile, yet she only gets weird, "Dixie cup" riddles for emails?

(This email came from a full-time EMT)

HE: So you like making people laugh, huh?

ME: Beats the shit out of waiting for someone to get in an accident...

HE: Hi, how are you today, I like what you wrote, that you don't have kids or anything, also that your left front tooth sticks out further than your right, just like mine does, our mouths would fit good together

ME: Wow, no kids and crooked teeth! You've done wonders for my self-esteem. Like, destroying what little I had.

HE: Angels are not meant to be on a dating site what are you doing on here dear?

ME: I just clawed my way out of marriage Hell, and didn't realize I had stopped in dating Purgatory.

HE: So sorry to infringe on your privacy, but your charming profile is so resistible.

ME: Glad to know I'm so resistible! Reminds me of a little-known Star Trek quote, "Resistibility is infantile." ~Baby Borg

(Star Trek quote is NOT real. It was too resistible not to write.)

HE: Hello from the other side

ME: OMG!!! ADELE? I love you!!! Let's make musical, funny babies together!

HE: What?? This Butch. Who Adele?

ME: She's rolling in the deep!

HE: ?

ME: She loves chasing pavements

HE: you gotta dawg?

ME: We should set fire to the rain

HE: U into the outdurs

ME: Never mind, I'll find someone like you.

HE: U R a crazy b

ME: Rumor has it

HE: (blocks me)

ME: (breathes a sigh of relief)

HE: So what brought you to this site?

ME: There's a horrific food shortage and I'm looking for donations. All the men I know are tired of buying me dinner.

(Tampa is 20 miles from where I live)

HE: Ever travel to Tampa?

ME: Let me guess. Don't own a car?

HE: (blocks me)

(My friend "Barry" is trying to set me up with his friend, "Ben.")

BEN: I hope you had a great day. Barry tells me you're a good egg.

ME: Thank you, Ben. I'm a great egg especially if you like Easter Eggs. I'm colorful, I crack easily, and you'd better not forget where you hide me.

(From a profile with the name "Aloe-Sore-S-X.")

HE: wink wink

ME: you prick

(My response is over the top – but I did not like this guy's profile.)

HE: I see you're a comedian. You're on here for the jokes, aren't you?

ME: No… I'm here to find my one and only true love. My soulmate. That man who will bring me coffee in the morning, massage my feet, make me dinner and bring me red roses every night. That man who I can't wait to see walk out the door after breakfast. That man who comes home miserable after working his crappy, stress-filled $500k a year job. This Queen of Hearts wants to find her White Rabbit (or her Mad Hatter) while stumbling through Blunderland. Where is my Han Solo who believes there's nothing hotter than French kissing a She-Wookie? Where is my Prince Charming who would travel to a Holiday Inn Express and back to save his Snow White from a dwarf gang bang?

ONLINE DATING FUN #1

What others have to say about online dating...

"I am to online dating, what Thomas Edison is to the light bulb. I haven't failed 10,000 times, but I did find 10,000 men that don't work." ~Traci Kanaan, Comedian

---

"You can really see the differences in the level of fear going into online dating. Guys' number one fear with online dating is turning up at their date and the girl is a bit bigger than her picture – chubby. Whereas women's number one fear is that they're going to get murdered." ~Hampton Yount, Comedian

---

"It's right there in the name. It's not 'GreatCupid' or even 'GoodCupid.' It's OkCupid," ~Helen Hong, Comedian

---

CHEAP PICK-UP LINES

*You should sell hot dogs because you already
know how to make a wiener stand.*

I might as well call you "Google," because you have everything that I'm looking for. Cheap pick-up lines take a little more thought than Tire Kickers, but they're not original or honest. Their most redeeming feature is that they ooze with schmaltzy insincerity, like Las Vegas pinky rings and white loafers. Let's not forget the gold chain! Tire Kickers get an "F" for effort, Cheap Pick-up Line Artists get a "D" for "How you DOIN?"

HE: How are you beside so amazingly beautiful like every single day?

ME: It's easy! Those pictures aren't me.

- -

(I live in St. Petersburg, FL, but received this while I was working in Cleveland, OH)

HE: What brings you to Cleveland?

ME: An airplane.

HE: Is that a mirror in your pocket cause I see myself in those pants

ME: A mirror reflects. You should see yourself in your pants, and this is probably not new for you.

HE: If I had a photo of you, I'd send it to Santa so he would know what I wanted for Christmas.

ME: Damn! All I want for Christmas is someone to stuff my turkey.

HE: Either you stop being so attractive, or you chat with me. Your choice.

ME: Hitting myself with an ugly stick now...

HE: Do you have a map? Because I keep getting lost in your eyes!

ME: Thank you, but I only have one eye. The other is glass. Do you like to play marbles?

HE: You just don't look like someone I would meet online.

ME: You don't look like someone I'd respond to. Maybe we shouldn't meet?

HE: Hi! Saw you on here, and thought I'd throw my line in the water.

ME: Hi back! Drown your worm often?

(I had received about 10 messages over several days about how amazing this guy thinks he is...)

HE: Good morning we are still fishing maybe we should change our bait?

ME: Maybe we should quit fishing in the shallow side of the pond?

HE: Hello how are you doing there, my name is Rob and I'm a thief and I'm here to steal your heart

ME: Hello Rob, fellow thief here. Hand over the family jewels and no one gets hurt.

HE: Hey what is it like being the prettiest dang woman in the whole state of Florida?

ME: Well, it's a lot easier than being the prettiest dang woman in the whole state of California, but much harder than being the prettiest dang woman in the whole country of Lichtenstein.

(Received this while traveling in New Orleans)

HE: Hey good-looking cat got your tongue one lucky cat

ME: Cat got my tongue? No... I'm a voodoo high priestess. I have the cat's tongue. All I need to finish my magic potion to prevent bad dating karma... is the lips, two freckles and canned fart smell from any guy who utters "cat got your tongue." Let's meet tonight, midnight, under the full moon near the haunted cemetery.

HE: (blocks me)

HE: Want to meet me for a drink tonight?

ME: Some women take walk-ins, but I require reservations 48 hours in advance.

ONLINE DATING FUN #2

I felt like this book needed some redeeming features, like serious facts and figures about online dating. So, I googled "online dating facts" and copy-and-pasted shit from some of the first 5 listicles I saw. If it's online... you know it MUST be true.

83% of all online dating profiles contain a lie.

The other 17% of online dating profiles contain untruths.

Total number of single people in the U.S.: 54,350,000

Total number of people in the U.S. who have tried online dating: 49,650,000

Annual revenue from the online dating industry: $1,935,000,000

Average spent by dating site customer per year: $243

Average length of courtship for marriages that met online: 18.5 Months

Average length of courtship for marriages that met offline: 42 Months

Percent of users who leave within the first 3 months: 10 %

Percent of male online dating users: 52.4 %

Percent of female online dating users: 47.6 %

Percent of marriages in the last year in which the couple met on a dating site: 17 %

Percent of current committed relationships that began online: 20 %

Percent who say common interests are the most important factor: 64 %

Percent who say physical characteristics are the most important factor: 49 %

Percent of people who believe in love at first sight: 71 %

Percent of women who have sex on the first online dating encounter: 33 %

Percent of people who say they have dated more than one person simultaneously: 53 %

Percent of sex offenders who use online dating to meet people: 10 %

Okay. Done with redeeming features. Back to the funny shit.

FOOLS RUSH IN

I'm not impatient.
I just don't like to wait.

Some people are just a little too anxious to meet, and that's what this chapter is about. I get it, too. The "Lonelies" set in, you're tired of eating alone, you wish you had someone to wake up to, you wish more than anything that you could find the right person to annoy for the rest of their life, but NO. You've been dealt an entirely different hand, either by your choice or someone else's. They say, "Patience is a virtue." So relish in some of the emails I got where "patience" and other virtues became extinct.

HE: I want to meet you, and the sooner the better.

ME: The only day I have a little time free this week is Friday.

HE: My daughters and their families are arriving Friday to spend the Christmas holiday with me. Why don't you join us for dinner that night at my place?

ME: I can't really think of a first date that would be more awkward than meeting your entire family for a holiday dinner at your house.

HE: So Friday it is!

ME: Um... can I bring anything? Like a bodyguard, personal fire-arm, side dish of sarcasm?

HE: I love your profile! I'm coming over right now.

ME: Awesome! You can be the first to check out my new designer perfume, Peppah Spuray! It's by Selph Defenzz.

HE: So, have you worked me into your show?

ME: Oh yes. I've written hours of totally hilarious new material solely based on this email, and the other five emails you sent prior to this that all said "Hey." OMG – you loving long walks on the beach, candlelight dinners, and height weight proportional, fitness oriented, tall blond chicks who like motorcycles and love to fish is totally hilarious, not at all cliché and completely relatable to every girl who ever went on a date with a guy who posted 3 pictures of himself: one from elementary school, one from high school (with complimentary parachute pants and mullet), and one from "6 years ago" in front of your TransAm with your bestie pitbull. It's hard to believe a guy who makes $250k a year like yourself is still single and SO interested in me!!! I hope we meet soon. I've pretty much decided if I ever get an hour-long Comedy Central special, I'll spend every second talking about YOU and how amazing you really are.

HE: Hi how are you doing? My name is Randy and I am in Tampa. Sure would like knowing you better so how about we talk soon? What's your name? Better yet call text me OK 813-XXX-XXXX

(5 minutes later)

HE again: Like what I see let's talk soon!! Call text me 813-XXX-XXX hope hearing from you soon

(3 minutes later)

HE again: Let's talk soon!! Call text me 813-XXX-XXX OK

(About 5 more emails like these followed within minutes of each other)

(Next day)

ME: Wow!!! I just read your profile and emails and we are not a good match. You seem really clingy and I'm not, so I filed a restraining order as a precautionary measure. Nothing personal, I just feel that if anyone uses chloroform as an aphrodisiac, it's you.

HE: Hi i am completely new to the idea of open minded relationships and in truth it was my wife's idea. I don't want to waste your time so if you see my page and want to talk great ask anything . I am also sorry for the picture i don't take selfies really and that the on she put up I will add more at some point

ME: Well thank you for the inquiry, however, I'm rather closed-minded about open-minded relationships involving your wife. Regarding your picture? You are amazing hot, in a 1972 "hippie dropping acid" kind of way. I can see why she wants you to meet other women.

HE: I would love to massage your body.

ME: I hope you have long fingers, especially since you live in Ireland.

HE: I read your profile and your questions. I like you and i want you as soon as possible. So what next?

ME: You can start by replacing your profile picture with one of you that looks a lot less like a serial killer...

HE: Im "Allen," you've really caught my eye... .sorry, Im terrible at this. Lol. Think wed get along... .so please answer! Im not moving either, ignore that part! Lol. You're fricken insane... .too attractive. And please tell me that's your real body lol

ME: I don't know how to tell you this, but it's NOT my real body. I'm renting it from a less attractive person I met at the fricken insane asylum.

(I had to edit his email, as it was quite lengthy)

HE: Hello and how are you ? I'm "Jed" and it's so nice meeting you on the dating site and i felt it's important at this juncture to let you know who i am, White/Caucasian. I'm Self Employed Real Estate Agent with a Master Degree, I have a good sense of humor. I'm a widower and have been widowed for 5 yrs now. When i read through your profile i was really amazed and motivated to send you a message to show my interest in you for the reason that God lead me to you for a good and right reason and I hope we can both work good things out on here as my heart and soul desire you for whom you are

ME: Hi Jed! All I can say is, if God led you to me, he needed a really good laugh. Heaven must've had a slow news day.

HE: I am a guy who's comfortable in his skin also, you are absolutely beautiful (seconds later) Hot damn woman, you are a freak to, I'm so in love right now

ME: Why do I think you could make this more uncomfortable if you wanted to?

HE: Hi beautiful , how are you doing today ? I just joined this site and I'm here to meet a good woman that is ready to make a happy home with me .. You can text me on mobile number XXX-XXX-XXXX.

ME: OMG! Santa has answered my prayers! I've been wanting a permanent home for nearly 2 years, but I always get returned because of my heroin abuse and incontinence.

HE: Your lips lips and lips spoke to me! Grrr!

ME: Indeed my lips lips and lips were speaking to you! They were saying "Oh HELL NO!!!"

(First email from this guy... I swear.)

HE: Will you marry me?

ME: Wow. We skipped the blind date and went right to the blind marriage! I'll entertain your proposal. Just to let you know, if you think my dowry is 2 goats and a pregnant mule – THAT will be a huge deal breaker. I'm worth at least 3 goats and a 2-hump camel.

HE: Hello funny and quick witted woman! I read your profile and would TRULY love to talk with you and meet when you feel comfortable. I am open and genuine.

(And they lived unhappily ever after... because HE deleted his profile 15 minutes later.)

ME: It was great not knowing you!

(12:58am)

I read ur profile im so interested

I really interested plz message me bk

(9:29pm)

If your free id love to talk

(10:03pm)

Plz message me when u see this

(11:47pm)

I'm seriously excited I hope I hear from u

(11:50pm)

(User no longer has an account)

ME: Whew!

COUGAR COOKIES

An old woman who dates a much younger man is called a "Cougar." An old man who dates a much younger woman is called "Rich."

Cougar Cookies is my nickname for 18-30 years olds. They often hit up women like myself in their 40s-50s, because older women are more sexually experienced than women their own age. We've worked through all the hang-ups women in their 20s have. We realize time is short and best of all? The sex drive of a Cougar Cookie matches well with an older woman. But sometimes... the social inexperience of a Cougar Cookie offends the Cougar he is trying to attract... as shown below...

HE: I'm looking for an older woman to teach me how to fuck.

ME: You just called me older, and told me you don't know how to fuck. What's my incentive?

HE: I'm looking for a horny, wet mature woman who wants amazing hot phone sex with a sexy young stud. I'm laying in bed right now jerking this thick hard young cock wanna hear me moan for you?

ME: You type really well with one hand.

HE: Do you like young guys with big fat cocks?

ME: Honestly, I like old guys with big fat wallets a lot more. Seeing an oxygen tank and IV painkillers being carried by a Hospice employee is enough to make me orgasm.

HE: You are interesting, but so am I!!!

ME: Yes, you are interesting! And without a face pic, all I can say is those fine 6-pack abs with those red white & blue Trophy Boy jockey shorts didn't hurt your interestingness either.

HE: (26-year-old male) And so you know i like older women girls my age suck

ME: If girls your age suck, then I'm not sure why you think I'll do the same after you just called me older.

HE: My name's Lorenzo. I'm 26 and Italian, hope you don't mind accent, but i live in the USA now.

ME: Maybe Italy is different, but in the USA it's really hard to be bothered by an accent from someone who has only sent you one email. (Typed in my best South Jersey / Cajun CoonAss accent.)

(Received 12:58am from a "31-year-old Hispanic male" that looks like he's 18.)

HE: Business professional in town on a company paid for hotel. I have drinks and looking for company tonight. Want to play? I have party favors. In Tampa with booze and party favors. You can sleep in tomorrow while I'm at work.

ME: I'd love to, but I'm home watching *Pretty Woman* tonight. I'm in St Pete with booze, fuzzy slippers, and cats. When I get tired of looking at Richard Gere and want to switch to the Puerto Rican equivalent of Pee Wee Herman who's too cheap to hire an escort, I'll be sure to let you know.

(From "MILFHunterXX")

HE: Hey there :) You're hot! I'm 28... like younger men? We should skype. I like to stay a mystery but I promise I don't disappoint haha whats your skype screen name I'll add you?

ME: It's CougarCookieAnnihilator

HE: Wow, the women in their 40s especially you are way hotter than the 20 somethings

ME: Well, thank you! That's the nicest way I've ever been told I was old. :D

(From a 19 year old)

HE: I just had to write and tell you that for your age, you look amazing!

Me: Thank you. I just had to write you back and tell you that for your age, you look like jail bait.

(From a 27 year old, who has his cap on backwards in his profile pic, responds to one of my "Instant Deal

Breakers" that states I'd prefer a guy who is a 70% match or higher.)

HE: You actually think the match percentage is accurate?!?! Lmfao God help us all

His Profile: Love a woman with class. If you have floozie photo's I assume you have no self respect for yourself. I also assume you need a glass of water because thats thirsty as hell.

ME: OKCupid shows we are a 62% match. I knocked off 30% for your arrogance, another 30% for being a judgmental prick, and 2% for your stupid glass of water analogy. That makes you a total ZERO.

HE: Hey baby ??. I'm 21 & go to Usf. I really want a girl to dominate me for a day. I wanna be somebody's sex slave & be used to eat your oussy & Ass on command, suck your toes massage your back & feet & be forced to fuck again & eat you out again just to make you cum. Lmk if you want this boo ??

ME: You're an idiot. Boo-bye!

ONLINE DATING FUN #3

Things you should never say on a first date...

unless it's true, or you're me.

♦ You've been single awhile, haven't you?

♦ Of all the dates I've been on, you're the most recent.

♦ After meeting you, I'm pretty sure I don't want to get over my ex.

♦ I'm "almost" divorced. I can't get him to leave his house.

♦ I can't believe you swiped right on me. I'm totally out of your league.

♦ Oh that's right... my phone rang and I swiped right on you by accident.

♦ How much do you make? Oh shit. I'll never get out of debt if I date you.

♦ Is that your real hair color? No... I mean the hair on your back.

- Do you want to play charades? Just wondering, because your accent is annoying.

- What's the worst thing you've ever done? Seriously? You have a story that doesn't involve the po po?

- I have a date with someone else tomorrow, but I can cancel him if this goes well.

- Did you see our waiter? I'd so hit that.

- I showed my friends your picture and they approve.

- I need to be back home by 10pm. I have to catch up with my friends.

- I hope you don't mind, but I looked you up on Facebook…

- When was your last complete STD panel done?

- I know we just met, but I think I'm in love.

- What's your name again?

- I'm so sorry, I have to take this call from my ex.

- I never go on dates with guys who are hotter than me.

SPELL CHECK AND PUNCTUALITY ARE NOT YOUR FRIENDS

"The impotence of spell check cannot be strongly stated enough."

In a world where most people respond to everything with their cell phones, online dating responses are riddled with shortcuts, spell-check errors, and punctuation mistakes. If you are looking for someone who is educated and literate, emails are a great way to screen out "the haves," "the have-nots," and "the have knots."

I'm not really a grammar nazi (just ask my editor), but I found that a command of the English language (or obvious lack thereof) is a very convenient way to eliminate potential suitors, especially if you're looking for an educated companion.

If you're only looking for a hook up? Phuck it. Grammar don't matter. I'll admit that a person's command of the English language is not the greatest way to judge a person. Some of the smartest people I know have some serious personality flaws, and some of the nicest, most caring people I've met are not "book" smart. But taking a few minutes to know the most common spelling errors like knowing the difference between "your" and "you're" and "there," "their," and "they're" could save you from a permanent dating "time-out."

HE: I like ur profile. and the way u have ur words n ur profile.

ME: I have words in my profile so you can read them. Many guys have read these words and discovered I was not a good match for them. I hope you will do the same.

HE: Helo would love 2 love u help me help u

ME: Hi u can help me by not loving 2 love me after u send me 1 email

---

HE: Ho.

HE: Hi.

ME: OMG. Did you just misspell "Hi?" Maybe you're the dyslexic eighth dwarf from Snow White, who meant to say "Hi Ho?"

HE: Making fiends?

ME: Nope. They're already fiends by the time I get them.

(Day 1)

HE: Helo sexy

(Day 2)

HE: Im sapiosexual to. I have know problem buying you coffee

ME: (Traci's serious note: Definition of "Sapiosexual," is a person who finds intelligence sexually attractive or arousing.) (Traci's sarcastic note: Evidently, you can be sexually attracted to intelligent people, but not be one yourself. "No" what I mean?)

(Day 3)

HE: Why you no answer me

(Day 4)

HE: Every time you no answer me... I more attracted.

ME: Hi. I answer you. You be less attracted now.

HE: You remind me of the constipation, cause you're a national treasure Have a happy day pretty girl.

ME: Awww... what a sweetheart! I'll bet you always say the un-shittiest things. :D

HE: You ready sexxxy to get acquainted and be my babee and ladee?

ME: Ummm... NO. Spelling errors aside, I just feel a huge disconnect between what you wrote and your user name "SPIRITandFAITHinJESUS."

HE: hello cell I guess I should start off with a dirty joke can take it you hear about the new study about now all men are bisexual know by sex whenever they have to that one is from me so I'm (35) I am less than 50 miles away from you I'm from (Detroit) love doing the normal stuff that everybody says on this site just the whole body and that thing about flirting that you were talking about I miss signals all the time time and once I would be with somebody I'm not really interested in anything else I get caught up in my own little world sometimes but I'd like to get caught up in some lady I'm tired of being alone I want exclamation relationship I want someone to snuggle with hold her hand when she needs me this is me when I need it and loving it each other all the time if you're that girl I hope you can find it in your heart to choose me so I hope to hear from you your lovely lady and I'd like to have fun with a funny lady okay love to hear from you and kind of in personal all this texting it's hard to show emotion so if you'd like my phone number I'd be happy to give it to you and we could talk on the phone as long as you like alright I wish you a great day and goodbye,

ME: it appears we've both had hysterectomies as neither one of us seems to have a period

- -

HE: Not bad, however, your a little too sedentary for me

ME: That's quite all right. YOU'RE a little too illiterate for me.

- -

HE: How r u ? U sure r a very nice looking woman , keep up the good job

ME: thank u fer da lettrz of n cur age ment.

HE: what's up with the wonder woman outfit, I want to meet you I think I'm fun would like to go up against a pro... just be nice & don't make me cry let's talk and I mean talk texting is not my thang

ME: If you want to go up against something that will make a huge difference in your life, don't start with a comedian. Start with an English teacher.

HE: I like you s lot

ME: I like you d ick.

HE: nice twatts

ME: Just checking... did you mean nice TITS or nice TWAT?

70

ONLINE DATING FUN #4

More facts and figures that I copied and pasted from the internet. Just so we're clear, I have personally avoided verifying every one of these facts. Why? Because it doesn't matter. The only thing that matters is this book is funny, and that you feel better about why you're going to be single, miserable, and lonely for the rest of your pathetic life. Even if it's only for a few nanoseconds.

According to the U.S. Census, there are 95.9 million unmarried people in the U.S. of which 47% are men and 53% are women.

Traci says: "47% men" means there are 45,073,000 eligible single men. But after you subtract the 4.1% who are gay, the 6.6% who are unemployed, and the 89% who feel that most marriages won't last... your chances of living happily ever after, is less than 0.3%.

An attractive "About Me" section in your online dating profile often includes a brief description of what you are passionate about or thankful for, a couple of things your friends say about you, qualities you are looking for in a potential partner, the first thing people notice about you (other than appearance), how you spend your leisure time, five things you can't live without, and the latest good book you've read.

Traci says: Disagree. An attractive online "About Me" should include a man expressing tremendous interest in doing housework, going shopping with me, massaging my feet, and buying me flowers.

Choosing exciting places for a first date increases the chances of the other person falling for you. There is a definitive link between danger and physical/romantic attraction.

Traci says: I had a first date at a clothing optional resort. It was also our last date. There is a definitive link between danger and seeing someone naked too soon.

Studies show that happiness is contagious and that potential dates find it hard to walk away from happy people. One of the biggest turn-offs during a date is negativity.

Traci says: Negativity is a turn-off? Obviously written by some whiny, pathetic, pessimistic, sorry-ass loser.

Studies show that remembering bits of information about a person and working them into conversation is not only highly flattering but also shows interest.

Traci says: Who knew "paying attention" was sexy?

Typically, dating specialists suggest waiting until the third date to cook someone dinner at home.

Traci says: It is my personal policy to avoid cooking until my 5th wedding anniversary. Food poisoning is NOT sexy.

On average, daters will kiss on the second date.

Traci says: I try to kiss before the first date. This makes me above average.

Couples usually wait until 6 to 8 dates before they are willing to enter into an exclusive relationship.

Traci says: I've not had this exclusive relationship problem yet.

On average, it takes between 12 to 14 dates before couples will trade house keys.

Traci says: I have "smart locks" for my house. No more re-keying locks. I just change the code!

If a man can't decide what to wear on a date, he might want to wear blue. Studies show that women are attracted to men in blue.

Traci says: Great if you're dating police officers, but don't underestimate what "brown" can do for you. Hello UPS driver! Nice package!

Ninety-two percent of single parents would rather date other single parents.

Traci says: Good to know. 100% of single people without kids would rather not date single parents.

---

4 out of 10 workplace dating relationships result in marriage.

Traci says: What this study doesn't say, is that 3 out of 10 workplace dating relationships get someone divorced, 2 out of 10 get someone promoted, and 1 out of 10 get someone fired.

If you want to create an instant link with a date, say his or her name at least twice in the conversation. This shows attentiveness and connectedness.

Traci says: That's right, Dear Reader. If you say someone's name twice in a conversation, they'll like you more. You know what I mean, Dear Reader? I feel so close to you now, Dear Reader.

3x... BOOM!

Body type is important in attracting a date. Studies show that overweight individuals were perceived less favorably than thin or muscular people. Thin individuals were perceived as intelligent but fearful, and muscular individuals were perceived as being healthy, brave, and good looking.

Traci says: I like men with some meat on them. There's nothing worse than cuddling with a 2 x 4. If you're breakable, you're not fuckable.

Body language studies show that revealing areas of the body that aren't usually on display (such as the inner wrist, the inside of the upper arm, ankles, feet, inside calf muscle, and the nape of the neck) has an immediate effect on a date and shows an instant liking.

Traci says: Seriously, who came up with this bullshit research? You know what else shows an instant liking? Taking all of your clothes off.

Mirroring, or repeating someone's body language, often impresses a date because it subtly conveys interest to the other person. One should avoid copying every move, however.

Traci says: Mirroring, or repeating someone's body language is very uncomfortable if you're dating a mime, clown, or a porn star. Trust me.

FATAL TRANSACTION

(1:23am)

HE: So how do I start this out without sounding like the other corny replies you probably receive regularly and roll your amazing lioness eyes at before hitting the shitcan button? We are 96% a match, which is a new high score for me without even picking up a joystick, so congratulations! You won free tickets to today's ride and show pony dance where I am going to try and convince you that we may want to persue something we don't yet have. No I am not on one knee and holding a little box with a pretty bow on it. But hopefully if things go right you will have me on my knees in some shape or form. I saw your photo first and was sucked into your stare then realized holy shit 96%! Then read your profile and knew I needed to reach out to you. You are funny, cool, upfront and damnit, I feel like you totally get me and understand oh wait, you are a comedian. Of course I am nodding my head! Just kidding, that is an added bonus. I will admit I zoomed in on your bicep tats and those words screamed out to me. Very inspirational indeed! And your wings are out of this world sexy as hell. They remind me of my favorite line by Jim Morrison "Death makes angels of us all and gives us wings where we had shoulders, smooth as ravens claws. I touched her thigh and Death smiled." Not that I affiliate your wings with Death, lol but I think he liked flirting with death and he pictured Death as a sexy vixen like you and not some creepy grim reaper.

The pitcher looks at first, winds up and throws a fast ball... in a nutshell to get the basic bullshit out of the way.

42year old white male red hair, average build, 5'11" not your skinny jeans wearing hipster.

Benefits:

No Diseases
Never done Drugs
Non-Smoker
Never Married
No kids
Not batshit crazy
No criminal record
Works fulltime,makes good money
No Debt

Features:

Short hair up top
Hairy chest
Not so hairy down there (completely shaven)

Big Dick
Great hands
Wicked tongue
Sarcastic, smartass, witty, sense of humor

Ok now that I have hopefully proven that this is not bullshit and I legitimately want to persue this chase and follow you into the rabbit hole, I want to become at least an important gear in your clockwork and when it comes time for our cogs to meet again we maintain a healthy connection. If in the remote chance we connect and want more I do have a valid passport and a job I can do remotely as long as there is wifi and a cellphone signal. So if you required me to travel with you that could be done with some planning.

Outside of the bedroom I am an extrovert, socially accepted but not politically correct. I enjoy kayaking in intercoastal waterways and rivers, dining out, sleeping in, comedy clubs.

I don't want to overdo this. I am extremely interested. If you are interested and I hope you are, please let me know

(1:06pm)

ME: (reads the email while running errands, can't respond)

(1:08pm)

HE: (sees I'm online) Hello?

(1:11pm)

HE: Well, Fuck. Guess I didn't even get you to bat an eyelash. I knew it was a kinda like playing the carnival game, and you were the big teddy bear that I would have had to tie to the roof if I won, but I tried. I don't bruise too easily though. So where did I lose you at? Did you read it from start to finish? Was it too fucking long?

(2:12pm)

ME: You lost me on the whole baseball, carnival of death analogy. That and I hate redheads that come with a side of psycho. (Block)

BOOBS ON BOOBS

*"Boobs are proof that men really
can focus on two things at once."*

I have boobs. They're big. People notice them. I can't help it. People have always made fun of my boobs, since I started growing them at the age of 10. It wasn't until my 30s or 40s that I finally embraced my boobs in all their freakishly awesome "triple D" glory. However... not everyone in online dating has done the same. Some men are offended by boobs. When I published a few pictures of me in a corset (which is what I wear on stage when I perform), some of these men decided to tell me just how much it offended them.

HE: I see these pics of you sticking your boobs up in camera, or at angle so boobs show... ... .this isn't what i am looking for.I am a man, and ya we all look, but if you offer that right off the back, then you aren't for me... ... ..sorry... ... .lil old school, but I am who I am.

ME: Wow... thank you so much for your advice! Next time I get some pictures taken, I'll remember to take off my boobs and put them in storage so no one can see them. I wonder how many men are out there thinking "I'm so sick of boobs," and "Damn it, another boob pic!" and "Get those big bazoombas out of my face!" but just don't have your li'l old school self to coach me on this matter. Also, thank you for letting me know I'm not what you're looking for. Time well spent on your part.

HE: Meat department on sale, buy 1 breast get 1 free is this how u look for a gentleman? Wrong way lady

ME: Teeny Weenie Department! You have a call! If you're offended by my boobs, check out my profile on www.PlentyOfAmish.com.

HE: have you notice you have big tits?

ME: No shit! No wonder I'm having so much trouble typing you back with these big ol' titties in the way. It's a wonder I can see the computer.

HE: Holy shit tits, Batman!

ME: Well if it isn't my arch rival, Tater Tot Cock!

ONLINE DATING FUN #5

More things you should never say on a first date...
unless he's THAT clueless you're not a match. It's
time to step up your game so you can step on out!

♦ How's online dating working out for you?
  Because it sure isn't working for me tonight!

♦ I usually don't go for straight guys, but I could
  make an exception for you.

♦ I still live with my parents. It's only temporary,
  you know, until I can move in with you.

♦ OMG, my mom would love you. Her assisted
  living facility is right there, let's stop in! Don't
  worry, she has dementia. She'll never remember
  meeting you.

♦ Check out my new ankle bracelet! It was a gift
  from the po po.

♦ Let's meet at a clothing optional resort! My
  treat... What do you mean you've never been
  naked? That's not what your mom said... I mean
  when you were born.

- I've only been clean from heroin, crystal meth, and opioids about 2 months. That doesn't scare you, does it?

- Want to go to a strip club? My half-sister is working tonight and she owes me money.

- Are you gonna eat that? (I don't wait for an answer, and I just start eating whatever's on his plate.)

- You'd be perfect if you were 20 pounds lighter, had more facial hair, less back hair, weren't so bald, and had a personality.

- Oh shit. My husband just walked in.

- The tattoos on my arms I got in prison.

- I just found out I'm pregnant.

- I actually like living with my parents.

- You had HOW many sex partners? Why so few?

- Where's a good place for me to smoke some weed?

- Mind if I bring my butane torch? It's for "dabbing."

LIARS

They say, "Believe half of what you read, and none of what you hear." So if you read this chapter silently, half of it is still true. Pinky promise! I cannot tell a lie, these are actual letters I received via online dating. I would never lie to you about something so unimportant.

___

HE: Hello my name is Captain "Courage" Joe ,I am single and new on this site to search for my soulmate, I am here seeking a serious, honest,caring,dedicated and responsible Woman for a life term relationship. Am a Single dad with a daughter bearing Felicia ,I lost my lovely wife three years ago alcohol,irresponsiblity and more importantly,she is doing drugs.I was going through profiles and found yours interesting,thats why i contacted you i am interested in you and really want to get to know more about you i am from Texas El Paso fort bliss ,Usa, and i will look into relocation for a serious relationship...

ME: I think it's best you stay in Texas. I'm not sure my rampant addictions to heroin, opioids, meth, crack, crank, and compulsive lying are going to help your situation. In fact, I barely had time to write you in between doctor shopping, AA meetings, and moving out of my pimp's mom's house.

(From a guy with a profile that is something like JAMES_BOND_007)

HE: I'm on Mars but will return soon :)

ME: Wow. Who knew Mars had such good WiFi?

HE: Hi Am Sean by name. I am from Nigeria. I am a model artist. I explore the world for modelling and it's what I do for living. Few of the places have been around the world is USA, Turkey,France and Spain. Hi came by your profile and I was thrilled and couldn't bear not saying an hi to would be glad to know you better.Here is my whatsapp cell xxxxxxxxxx You can also sent me a request on facebook or instagram.

ME: OMG! I'm a fictitious model from Nigeria too! You must be big time! I've only been to Canada, Mexico, and a few remote parts of Oklahoma. We should definitely exchange pics we stole from other people off the internet.

HE: I was stopped by the police today! The officer came up to me and asked if I knew what the reason was, and I answered "no idea officer". He said it was because of texting and driving! Then I pulled up my phone showing a picture of you to explain my cause. He looked at me for a long time, thinking. But let me go at the end, understanding my situation, but expected me to get you into this convo!!

ME: How exciting! Happy to join your convo. Do you think you being in The Czech Republic will be an issue? Maybe I can Uber...

CANDIDLY CREEPY, WILDLY WEIRD

"Give a man a mask and he will become his true self."

These are the emails I received from men that make me shake my head, cringe in horror, and ponder the positives of chemical castration. Why would anyone write this shit? As a single woman, there's always that chance I have a date with a serial killer, but at least these guys gave me advance notice. Thank you from the bottom of my ice cold, cynical comedy heart.

HE: You know what I'd do with you?

I'd dress you up in black leather head to toe because you're the bad one and I'd dress you in white leather head to toe because you're the good one. Then I'd take you in my space ship, we'd travel the galaxy and you'd be my space princesses. And then when we'd come back to earth we'd make all the girls jealous.

ME: I'm just not interested, Tom Cruise...

(Sigh. From a random guy who read several of my other online dating posts on Facebook, and decided to throw his hat in the ring.)

HE: So before i pursue this any further, would you be interested in me as a friend with benefits? If not its all good. But i am also attracted to you and thought maybe we could kick it up a bit.

ME: Your interest is much appreciated... but you are a little far from me (2-hour drive). It also appears you're already in a relationship with your wife, and I'm not interested in being your dirty little secret.

HE: Ok i understand. No problem. I am a bad boy though. Lol

ME: Obviously... if you're pursuing me when your wife just left on a business trip.

HE: Oh no i would pursue you anytime. Today is just a coincidence. I'll do it again on Monday when she is home. LOL

ME: (Douche!)

HE: Hello love the profile. I use to work for the Government I had to retire with Disabilities from an auto accident. I had 7 back surgeries. I am walking fine everyth Ing else works on mh body as well. Inf uou get the point. Lol. No but for real I am doing good. The only thing is I can't have any more children not that I need them mine are growing. I do get two checks a month. I do ok fof mh self. I manage fine. I am a very independent person I do not or will not ask any one to support me. I manage on my own. I am a very passionate person I do believe when you are in a relation ship you should be with that one person only. I do not like liares ,cheaters, arguing or fighting. Life is to short for the petty stuff. I am a bit old fashion I still know how to treat a women with respect. Open car doors helped them be seated in a restaurant or were evre you are setting down to eat. Yes mam please and thank you goes a long ways. I still suprise them every now and then with little supriese s.i believe you shoul walkwith your arms around each other in public or holding hands or even kissing and hugging you should show each other the true love you feel for each other. I feel that I have the most amazing woman in the world and I love her with all my heart I want every person I see that i am proud of what I have and want to show it off.

ME: Anything else I should know before I block you?

HE: Daddy likes what he sees honey

ME: Oh great! Just what I need! Another van without candy.

HE: I'd luv to get you drunk sometime

ME: Oh yeah? Well I'd luv to slip you a roofie and sell your organs on the black market.

(1 day, no response)

ME: Too soon?

SERIOUSLY SAPPY

"Being a hopeless romantic with a sarcastic mind is pretty exhausting."

As I write this lofty passage, rose petals blow sweet kisses to my delicate toes as sunshine-laced goblets of ruby red wine fill my longing jaws with quiet numbness. I long for the vintage days when the following mournful poems from the hearts of lonely mortals were written on lace handkerchiefs, in blood, to show their true affection to the hopefully, potentially betrothed.

Oh woe is me... those days of iambic pentameter, thrusting thy tortured souls onto swords of steel, and drinking magical elixirs to thy poisoned lips are no more. They have been replaced by the brilliance of Control+C and Control+V (the magic potion also known as "Copy" and "Paste") with only a CAPTCHA to hinder the progress of nanoseconds of thoughtless provoking work.

Seriously, when I get emails like these, I begin to wretch. I know somewhere, there's a poor greeting card writer being held hostage, bound and gagged in a storage room closet of an old abandoned elementary school. His captors are forcing him to consume gallons of coffee and sugar cubes, tickling his feet with feathers until he writes things that a self-respecting Harlequin romance reader would completely reject. Every time a woman doesn't respond to this drivel, the greeting card writer takes a slap to the face like a pimp punishing the ho who stole his money.

HE: I like your smile LOL I like a girl who smiles LOL Do you smile all the time? LOL

ME: No, I don't smile all the time. LOL When I get emails like this, I stop smiling because it interferes with my wincing and need to face palm. LOL

- -

HE: Is there such a thing as Loving To much??? Do you like getting morning flowers? Do you like having songs dedicated to you? Do you like a sense of security of a strong man with you and knowing However and When ever you "want it" it's yours for the taking. Would you mind getting a random call just to say I Love you? Do you believe romance is still alive but it's up to Us to continually feed it and add the Passion? If you answered yes to these and can add to this, then we should talk. I firmly believe we were not put on this 3rd rock from the sun to be alone. All replies will get a response. Let's make it a great day!

ME: Wow. I was going to suggest we see a movie, but couldn't decide between *Princess Bride* and *Fatal Attraction*. Ever get that email that leaves you with an impersonal, unrealistic creepiness that you just can't put your finger on? Boom! That's you. Meanwhile, I'm looking at houses on the 4th rock from the sun. Men are definitely from Mars.

HE: I apologize for my audacity when I speak to you, but I am a man who believes it would be a crime to see a woman as beautiful as you and not to say something beautiful, The beauty of a woman must be seen in her eyes, because that is the door of her heart, the place where love resides. My queen if your heart is as beautiful as your eyes you are a wonderful woman ... Hello how are you I hope you liked my words greeting

ME: Ummm... I sing dick jokes in comedy clubs for a living. If there is a door to my heart, I'm pretty sure it's not some barn stall you just shovel shit like this into.

HE: You are such a beautiful woman,i wonder why a beautiful woman like you is so single, I would love too know everything about you if you dont mind and i am looking for a woman who can be my Queen forever,a woman that complete me.,I go too church alot hope you dont mind about that,I am a career minded individual am looking for a woman who knows what she want and who does'nt play games.Am new here am searching for Some one who wants only one man forever and ever in her life.I am looking for that woman who i can be with forever and ever telling me more about you... i dnt stay on here you can text on here (xxx) xxx-xxxx... Looking forward to know you more better

ME: Sorry for the delayed response... I was playing Cards Against Humanity with 5 hot little Cougar Cookies across the street from the Westboro Baptist Church and the White Card was "Clingiest, Most Idealistic Guy You'd Never Date" and there was your email! I know you want to know more about me, but if you actually read my very complete profile, you'd have figured out by now I have men like you for a mid-afternoon snack.

HE: When walk by the sea ,what do you hear? When stars shine bright do they smile at you?? Do the tears for like rain and get gather in a jar? A smile will only last if the heart receive it.. Love is the strength of the world,just have to grab it and hold on!! Peace in the heart brings wonder.. Joy being a smile. Life is a a gift that should never be lost. Hold, grab it never let it go... For a lost soul is a lonely place.. Smile don't give up on LOVE it's are great gift... Pain and hurt only make us stronger. But never turn away from life for pain,hurt.joy happiness are all part of Life... A ying/yang. Nice to meet you and your profile touched my soul.

ME: Wow! Thanks for your "original" email. It was so nice to read every sappy, pedantic Hallmark greeting card while cringing in awkward exasperation from the comfort of my own home. Had my profile touched your eyes instead of your "soul," you would have more accurately concluded that I'm more of a Shoebox Greetings girl. But that's okay. You only get one chance to make a good first impression, and you blew it. Smile! Confucius say, "Jesus loves you."

HE: I really hope you wont think me too forward... But youre so far beyond stunning ♥ I would give anything to make you my Goddess... To bury my face between your thighs and worship you until youre trembling... Then id press you against the wall and kiss a loooong slow trail up the back of your legs...lingering just a moment where your thighs meet your ass ♥ then id push your legs apart and slide the,length of my throbbing shaft deep inside of you, holding still a moment so you feel me throb in reaction to your body ♥

ME: No. That's not too forward at all! I'll admit it's pretty advanced for a first email, kind of creepy and stalker-ish in some respects, and a little on the cheap and predictable side of a shitty romance novel but only in the nicest "copy and paste before you edited it" kind of way. But I wouldn't call it "forward."

STOOPID PEEPS

"When you are dead, you don't know that you are dead. It is difficult only for the others. It is the same when you are stupid." ~Anonymous

I gotta give these guys some credit for trying to open the conversation, but DAMN. Sometimes it just doesn't go as planned for them. Some guys are trying to be smart, some guys are just thoughtless, some guys are just rude. Why they feel compelled to write me I'm not sure. Why I feel compelled to write back... I'll never know.

HE: How daring are you on a scale from 1-10?

ME: I'm a 9. I'm not afraid to write and tell you this is the dumbest thing I ever read, but I'm not brave enough to give you my phone number.

HE: A well constructed profile. Permit that I ask if you are taken?

ME: Ummm... you sent the above note through an ONLINE DATING SITE, and my well-constructed profile says I'm DIVORCED and SINGLE in like 3 places. If you need more clues, Scooby Doo, I can get you a scary mask and a confession from old man Withers at the haunted amusement park.

HE: What's happening, The pursuit of pleasure is your personally NICE.. Would you say you are less agreeable, maybe more neurotic? Thought. Alone time your not into? Do what u like-I follow that also. Ring me back CYA

ME: My neurotic, less agreeable self decided she will best find happiness by leaving you alone. Word.

HE: Let's chat on Skype. Do you have a few minutes?

ME: Sure. (He finds my profile, and sends me a friend request, then nothing.)

ME: (I initiate a video call. He doesn't answer.)

HE: (Texts me through Skype) I meant TEXT chat, not VIDEO chat. I can't video chat.

ME: VIDEO chat is the whole point of Skype, you moron. We can SEE each other. Just a hint... this is much easier to pull off when you are who you say you are. And here I was all done up in my sexy Costco lingerie in hopes of convincing you I was an 18-year-old, high-dollar Swedish escort looking for a sugar daddy. What a loser!!!

HE: Even though you never got back to me... I still think you look amazing!

ME: Since you never wrote me before, you won't be disappointed when I don't get back to you again.

HE: I like board games and role play. Do you?

ME: I don't know. Your profile specifically said, "Don't contact me if you're a player or into games," so I'm not sure how to answer this.

(Read this message while running errands.)

HE: Good morning! How are you?

(Sees me online, and writes this message...)

HE: No peeking without speaking! LOL

(Several hours later)

ME: No jerking while I'm working!

HE: Wow hey sexy! You look like alot of fun! i dont mean to be rude or anything but have you ever been pounded by a big black cock before?

ME: Oh hey there, big guy! I don't mean to be rude or anything, but you have you ever been fucking bitch slapped by an Arab-Italian broad for writing stupid ass emails like the one you just sent me?

An actual conversation with a guy I went out on ONE date with. It will help if you read the "HE" voice in the worst Long Island, NY accent you could possibly imagine.

ME: I don't think we should see each other anymore.

HE: So, why don't yous want to go out with me again?

ME: Maybe because after ONE date, you watched every one of my youtube videos 5 times, and then you claimed me as your girlfriend on social media.

Then, you sent me several pics of you licking other women's private parts as well as pics of your dick with cum all over it. You've texted me every morning at 3am wanting to know what I was up to, because you don't seem to understand that I could be SLEEPING. Not to mention you're constantly interrup...

HE: What? Who yous talking about? You make me feel all dirty and bad about myself. What kind of girl does that? I'm the best friend you could ever have. I'm a gentleman. You're nuts. I don't know who you're talking about.

ME: (Block)

ONLINE DATING FUN #6

Trivia, again from the world's most trusted
reference book... the internet.

Speed dating, invented by a rabbi from Los Angeles in 1999, is based on a Jewish tradition of chaperoned gatherings of young Jewish singles.

Traci says: Speed Naked Dating is quite fun as well. If you don't like what you see, it's going to change soon enough.

The most common time for breakups is around three to five months.

Traci says: Silly me, I thought the most common time for breakups was right before Valentine's Day, Christmas, and my birthday.

Women who post a photo on Internet dating sites receive twice as many email messages as women who don't.

Traci says: No SHIT!!! People who see a photo of what they're buying are more likely to buy what they're seeing than people who don't see a photo. Researchers can be really fucking stupid.

One study found that men who reported incomes higher than $250,000 received 156% more email than those with $50,000.

Traci says: Again, NO SHIT!!! It takes the same amount of effort to blow a rich guy as it does a poor guy. What does any woman have to lose by contacting rich guys?

On free dating sites, at least 10% of new accounts are from scammers.

Traci says: It seems the other 90% of new accounts delete their profile within 3 days.

Thirty-three percent of online daters form a relationship, 33% do not, and 33% give up.

Traci says: I guess this sounds better than stating 66% just say "Fuck it."

If a group of women are standing together but their eyes are wandering, they are likely to be looking for guys. If they each take a turn to break away from the group to head to the bathroom alone, they are on the prowl. If they are huddled together giggling, they are usually not interested in finding men.

Traci says: Women wolf pack behavior, explained.

Depending on the type of women a man would like to meet, he should visit that type of clothing store. For example, if a man likes "outdoorsy" women, he should go to an outdoor clothing store.

Traci says: I shop at Macy's. Why do I keep meeting gay men?

The appropriate time to call after meeting a man or woman is hotly debated among dating experts. Typically, the ideal time to wait to call is two to four days, though no longer than four to five days. Calling too soon can appear desperate.

Traci says: I hate this. If you want to be with someone, call them. If you don't want to be with someone, don't call them. Don't let some dating expert yuck on your yum because it's too soon.

If a woman is interested in her date, she will often smile at his jokes, play with her hair, fidget with an object such as a glass, blush when he pays her a compliment, pout or pucker her mouth, stumble over words, or lean in towards him.

Traci says: She will also pinch his nipple, grab his ass, and say stupid shit. Oh wait... that's just me.

Beautiful women typically get more stares, winks, and harassment than average-looking women do, but they are also less likely to get asked out by average-looking men because those men tend to be intimated by them.

Traci says: I'm sorry, researchers. We're missing the question, "Why would a beautiful woman want to get asked out by average looking men?" Yea, I didn't think so either.

When a man first approaches a woman, she will base 55% of her initial impression of him on his appearance and body language, 38% on his style of speaking, and 7% on what he actually says.

Traci says: 100% of this is done in 30 seconds or less.

Dating specialists suggest that if a woman doesn't return a call after two messages, she is not interested.

Traci says: That is correct, and that does not change with additional calls.

It is hard for a man to strike up a conversation if there are just two women at a social scene because he doesn't want the other friend to feel abandoned. So a woman who is looking to attract a date should bring two "wing women" with her.

Traci says: Bullshit. Men see three women and think about banging all three, not banging one while the other 2 talk amongst themselves.

A recent AOL survey says that 40% of women view an appropriate time frame to wait for sex as being one to three months, while 35% of men think the third date is fine. On average, couples have sex within about 4 to 6 dates.

Traci says: Disagree, and perhaps I'm a bit more sexually liberated than most. Why are people waiting for sex? If the guy (or gal) is a lousy lay, no one wants to spend 3 months waiting for that newsflash.

If a woman offers to pay for everything, chances are she isn't that into the date. There's an unspoken understanding that a man paying for everything is a form of "copulatory gift," which is almost universal in all animal species.

Traci says: Copulatory Gifts are universal in all animal species? This is bullshit. If a male squirrel offers to buy a lady squirrel an acorn, she's not going to feel obligated to have squirrel sex with him. Mostly because she's a squirrel, and being easily distracted is what squirrels do for a living.

Over 50% of all singles in America have not had a date in more than two years.

Traci says: Don't feel bad. Over 50% of singles cheese slices have not had a date in more than two years either.

Research shows that men know they're falling in love after just three dates, but women don't fall in love until date 14.
Traci says: Date 14? I call "Shenanigans." When you've met as many men as I have, you fall in love on date 3 and hope it's still there by date 14.

29% of Americans have had sex on the first date.

Traci says: Shouldn't this be an even number?

Talking to a bartender makes a woman seem more friendly and makes it easier for a guy to jump in on her conversation.

Traci says: I swear if you get between me and my bartender, you're going DOWN.

A woman can increase the likelihood of a man approaching her if she uncrosses her arms, makes subtle eye contact, and smiles.

Traci says: It's called "letting your guard down."

Humans like mystery and "the chase," so don't be too "available" to a date. Dating experts typically suggest not sleeping too early with a date because the longer the chase, the more likely love will blossom.
Traci says: That explains why Scooby Doo is popular, but doesn't explain why Fred never screwed Daphne or Velma.

HONESTY IS NOT ALWAYS THE BEST POLICY

"The most free person is the one who has nothing to hide."

This chapter is dedicated to the few, the proud, and most honest people online. I wish everyone was this honest. It makes things so easy. You know instantly whether or not you want to be with them. In most of these cases you may not want to be with them... but at least you know before shelling out for dinner and drinks.

HE: I live in Illinois but in Tampa tonight. Looking for someone to go on a date, show me around, that sort of thing. If this would interest you, just let me know. If not and you would rather not talk to me, I understand.

ME: You didn't plan ahead, you want me to drop what I'm doing to be your Tampa tour guide AND you're a bit passive aggressive? 3 strikes, buddy. YOU'RE OUT!!!

HE: Like yo chat get to know more about you if you don't mind. My name is "Paul" Iam 50yrs old just lost my wife 2 weeks ago to cancer. She was 46yrs old. Trying to pick my self up and meet new people.

ME: Sorry to hear you lost your wife. What took you so long to date?

His Profile Name (altered to protect his identity): TyroneNeedSome

His tagline: wants women who likes bald black men

His interests: meeting different white beautiful women

His message to me: How are you doing beautiful

My response: I'm good. Who wouldn't be thrilled to find the most honest person in the history of online dating? It's so nice to finally be judged for the color of my skin, and not the content of my character.

(Guy who looks like a stereotypical biker)

HE: Ironic hashtagger. Emoji poet. I'm Chill as a chincilla. My partner and me are totally amazeballs cool. Q: Will there be drama? No drama from this Llama.

ME: MY profile is lengthy, well thought out, well written, grammatically correct, and no South American animal analogies. Yet, somehow we are a 97% match. Does this make me super awesome like a possum, or socially clunky like a monkey? This Honey Badger don't scare, or care, or dare date dat care bear...

(emoji haiku, bitches)

Profile from a Jamaican woman.

No Fbuddies If you brush with jewelry cleaner that's a no.. If you need instructions on how to wear a belt that's a no.. if you do not in possession of car , apt/home , job or no collective goals you are trying to get attained that's a no to

When my mother was in an assisted living facility, I enjoyed flirting with the male residents there. "Lester" was one of my favorites. He was in his 80s, wheelchair bound, and loved doing magic tricks for the ladies.

Lester motions for me to stop.

I stop.

He motions that he has something important to tell me.

I lean over (in my low cut t-shirt).

Lester: "You're BUILT... REAL... NICE."

ME: (Blushes. He got me. A compliment is a compliment, I don't care how old you are.) Thank you, Lester, for making my day!

FREAKY, SWINKY & KINKY

"Don't be ashamed of who you are.
That's your parent's job." ~Anonymous

I mentioned earlier that I do comedy for nudists, swingers, and BDSM people... or what I refer to as "sexually adventurous adults." It's kind of a weird niche. For the first time ever, I actually feel safer telling people my sexual preferences over my political preferences. I'm not a Democrat or Republican. I'm just a swing voter!

In order to keep up on the events I can provide comedy for, I have dating profiles on several swinging and fetish sites. Yea, that's it... to keep up on events for work. ;) Okay... so I'm a freak, and how nice would it be to find someone who could fully appreciate my freakiness?

In any event, I get some interesting inquiries from the general public just because I'm a single woman. But when you add the nudist/swinger/BDSM factor into things? You're bound to attract some freaky, swinky & kinky people. Here are some of my favorites!

HE: I love a woman that takes control.

ME: Then you shouldn't have written me first...

HE: Might you care to have some fun with a feisty, older guy like myself? BTW – I was referring to adult sexual fun

ME: Thank you for the explanation. I wasn't sure what you meant, with a profile name like "IWannaSpawnUntilDawn696969."

HE: I'd fuck you so hard.

ME: Well, it really doesn't work if you fuck me soft now, does it?

(Traci's note: FetLife.com is a social networking website like Facebook, only it connects people who are into BDSM, kink, and fetishes.)

HE: How kinky are you from a scale of 1-10

ME: Show me your Fetlife.com profile, and I'll tell you.

HE: What's Fetlife.com?

ME: If you are not even aware of one of the largest social networking BDSM sites, then I am a 37.

This inquiry came through fetlife.com as well.

HE: Ultimately, I'm looking for a slave or submissive.

ME: You did see "DOMINATRIX" in my screen name?

HE: Yes! I did see that and thought you would be a fun person to hang out with. I'm okay with that.

ME: If we were to get along, and I wanted to be your sub, what would that entail?

HE: Well, there's a training period of 60 days. I'd have you run my errands for me, hold my light when I read before bedtime, and as a reward, I might use you for a coffee table.

ME: Can't we just fuck? You could use my vagina for valet parking.

HE: (no answer)

ME: (just as well)

HE: Hi Traci, Not sure what to say, except that I'm just a dirty old bastard. I make 50 Shades of Grey look like Dr. Seuss.

ME: Oh wow... I'm really excited to meet you! I just got back from performing at a gay leather BDSM conference, and took classes on Strangulation & Asphyxiation, Orgasm Denial with Cock Cages, and Anal Fisting. I've been looking for a play partner.

HE: Ummm... You might be a little advanced for me...

ME: "Look at me! Look at me! Look at me NOW! It is fun to have fun... But you have to know how..." ~Dr. Seuss

HE: (blocks me)

HE: I'm into Taboo play.

ME: Like what?

HE: Role play.

ME: What kind of role play?

HE: Well... I like fantasizing about having sex with my imaginary sister.

ME: (no answer)

Next day.

HE: Am I too naughty for you?

ME: (no answer)

Next day.

HE: I'm too naughty for you aren't I

ME: (no answer)

Next day.

HE: I'm too taboo for you

ME: (no answer)

Next day.

HE: Don't you want to play with your dirty brother?

ME: No. I checked your references and your imaginary sister told me you were a lousy lay.

HE: I'm a gay guy looking to make some female friends.

ME: Just what I need! Another dick that's off limits.

HE: Are you into anal?

ME: Is your net worth $5 million?

HE: WTF? I'm 21.

ME: Not into anal.

HE: WOW. 98% Match we should get together
(I read his profile....)
HIS LIKES: Dominant guy that's willing to do whatever you want as a weekend sex slave. Bi-sexual, but only with female genders. You know who you are. Please no males. Transexuals, Hermaphrodites, and She-Males.
ME: I guess you missed the part in my description where I didn't say I wasn't a chick with a dick.

HE: Hi nice pics! you interested in a Gangbang with German guys?

ME: Sure, but only if they're angry German guys. I only like sour Krauts.

HE: I read EVERY word of your profile and am completely intrigued. I'd spank you every day of the week if I could.

ME: If you think you're going to spank me even one day of the week... I suggest you put "911" on speed dial. You're going to need it.

("ENFP" is a reference to my Myers Briggs personality type)

HE: 2-3 things? Really? Thsts absurd! We are so alike we may he incompatable. Is sex with your intellectual twin masterbation or incest? ENFP, no filter, not suitable for minors, Waffle House (at 3am), 25 year/million mile traveller ... oh shit go read my rambling *100% positive* profile. And as for proving my pictures current, I'll give you my fb id ... if you send me a selfie wearing naughty librarian glasses. At age 55 I got rid of my 2 cars. I gave one to my ex- and gave the other to my son. I ride around town on a giant red scooter. (wearing a red helmet, red jacket, red gloves and I bought 10 pairs of red shoelaces that I swap into new shoes when I buy them). If that is a deal breaker, just say so because for hot ENFP sex (the best!) with a quick witted foul mouthed musician comedian, I'll go buy a car. Actually I'd go steal a car, but that too is a "deal breaker" on your commandment list. Moses Shmoses! Jews had it easy.

ME: I didn't think there was one man that could make every other man on this site look absolutely amazing, but you've done it. Congratulations! I just wanted you to know that before I block you, I've left a Sugar Babies candy wrapper trail to a dumpster and issued my own Amber Alert.

HE: Ask me anything!

ME: What are your views on ethical non-monogamy and polyamory?

HE: It's wrong and I want nothing to do with it.

ME: You're going to burn an eternity in Swinger Hell just for saying that.

Subject: Fun for you:BBC;Thick and large head:

Hello:I imagine and anticipate You possess all he fruitful assets to consume. Allow me to engulf all the tender and delicate components of your scrumptious body, starting with a kiss on the fore head and our lips melting together like a grilled cheese sandwich.Let me massage your soft neck with light kisses and couple the nipples of your large breast into one and suckle them until you feel the warmness of my lips.Allow me to navigate my tongue around your abdomen,searching for your precious navel and then suddenly dropping to to the inner sanctuary of your large thighs that safeguard your vaginal treasure which I will invade with my soft fingers and open for insertion by my flickering tongue.I will tantalize your hot vagina until the heat produces the clitoris and batter the clitoris until the doors of your GSPOT expand and prepare you for insertion by my concrete penile rod flavor bringing volcanic orgasmic eruptions throughout your inner soul. I will be relocating to your area shortly

ME: Grilled cheese sandwich, vaginal treasure, and battered clitoris all in one email? Did you get all those from the same dick-tionary?

ONLINE DATING FUN #7

Even more things you should never say on a first date... unless you're pissed you chose this date over a medically-induced coma, and now you're not sure you know the difference between the two.

- ◆ OMG. That belt is working overtime.

- ◆ Oh my goodness. You are PERFECT!!! Let's stop in this jewelry store, I want to show you a ring I like.

- ◆ My 5 kids loved your pic and want you to be their dad.

- ◆ Are you neutered?

- ◆ You don't look nearly as good in person as you do in your pictures. I suggest you buy enough drinks until you do.

- ◆ How many sexual partners have you had?

- ◆ So you've never been arrested? Not according to what I found in the county records.

- ◆ My church is having a revival tomorrow night. Want to go? You could use some saving.

- You remind me so much of my daddy. He used to hold my hand like that.

- What happened to your ass? It's not there.

- Give me a second. I need to check in with my parole officer.

- I never thought female comedians were that funny.

- Who did you vote for in the last Presidential election?

- This place is expensive! Are you paying for dinner?

- Who's that text from? Your ex-girlfriend?

ASSHOLES

"I don't need you.
One asshole in my pants is plenty."

Every site has them. Dating sites have more than most. Trolls that want to tear you down. Posers that postulate. Spammers that spin lies. Their life sucks worse than yours, and by golly, they're going to do everything they can to bring you down to their level. Not today, assholes, not today. Your ASS is MINE.

HE: Hi

(I review his profile, and decide we are not a good match. I do not respond to his email.)

(He sees I reviewed his profile, then sends me a picture of a rose.)

HE: I sent you this rose... because you didn't like me.

(I send him a picture of a cinder block)

ME: I'm sending you this big ol' BLOCK because I like you less than I didn't before. (And... block.)

(This guy decided to make this comment regarding a pic I had of myself wearing Ren Faire attire.)

HE: are u just gonna peek or do you want the whole show,lol? I could use a medieval wench to fetch my mead and other things

ME: You think you're smart and so divine

But to me you're nothing more than swine

If we meet, wear your jock strap

This lovely wench won't take your crap

HE: Hey ya big nuthead! I see yer online...

ME: You mean, you SAW me online... aaaaaand BLOCK.

(Nobody calls Baby a "nuthead.")

(First date with this guy went well. Then he decided to micro-manage what was to be our second date.)

HE: We're going to "Coolah Cafe," be there by 5:06pm sharp, don't be late. It's outdoors, so be prepared for the hot weather. Make sure you eat a snack before dinner, because you're going to be trying the kava and a few other assorted drinks I've picked out and I don't want you to get too bombed. Also, make sure you wear a dress that shows off those fabulous breasts of yours, and no panties.

ME: Cool. Since we're passing out expectations, I'd like you to eat a peanut butter, bologna, and garlic bulb sandwich before we meet and do not bring breath mints because I'll be looking for reasons not to kiss you. No liquor and no 420, as we're going to be driving separately so I don't have additional reasons to run late. Make sure you wear a tight, hot pink thong that constricts your nut sack, and definitely wear white see-through pants so I can make sure you're just as uncomfortable as I'll be on our date.

(Date with micro-manager was canceled.)

(From a man living in Jamaica)

HE: Evening Queen, if every woman need the same guy and that perfect guy is on earth you don't think he wouldn't be hiding from you "lovely loyal women" sigh Human just need to stop search for someone to make them happy and start search for someone that they going to make happy.. And a next thing... Maybe the guy that have a nice personality and is your soulmate have a ugly face so you keep turn him down same way you will do me... .. Not saying you're the most beautiful woman.. Because we all have our fault... Your head a little big, but cute lol

ME: Let's see... did I reject you because you said my head was a little big, or because dating someone who lives in Jamaica is cost prohibitive?

- -

(This guy sends me an email, and we chat on the phone for a bit. Something told me we were not compatible, but I go ahead and set up the meeting with him anyway. I text him the next day to confirm.)

HE: I need to get back with you, I am still at work

(I was hoping he was blowing me off, and relieved he couldn't make it. I didn't give him another thought, until he texts me around 11:30pm that night)

HE: Yeah I wanted to meet up but I got out of work late, went home and fell asleep. If you want come by I will answer the door naked, if you like cum in

(I'm thinking this is pretty rude, seeing as how he didn't even officially cancel our meeting, reschedule, or apologize for the inconvenience. Then he expects me to show up for a booty call?)

ME: No thanks.

(3 hours later... now 2:30am)

HE: Yeah, I prefer girls in a little better shape! I am not gonna waste my time with you!

(I was going to let this go... but couldn't.)

ME: And I prefer guys that are a lot more courteous and considerate about canceling a date, and know how to treat a woman with respect.

HE: Oh well make a dick joke because you won't get a dick hahaha!!! If you wAnt I will charge 350.00 for an hour. I will fuck the Shit out a you. Loose my number.

7:35am

(Clearly, a "jenius." The next morning, I take pictures of all my sex toys, and send them to him. 25 photos.)

ME: Before I lose your number, I just wanted you to know I was able to outsource some dick for less than $10 an hour. They all showed up, on time, loved me for who I was, and they were, surprisingly, more interesting to talk to than you. When it came down to "business," they all patiently waited for me to finish, made sure I was completely satisfied, and then left me the Hell alone.

HE: I'm not into sending hatemail, but your profile and what you're "looking for" is incredibly negative and judgemental... Like your shit doesn't stink. If you're so perfect, why are you on here? Don't return this message with a stupid comeback; just block me. And figure out why you're alone right now.

(I blocked him, as requested.)

So you know... here is my incredibly negative & judgmental criteria.

Please pass me by if...

You and I are less than a 70% match. (I've found the match % to be pretty spot on, when someone fills out the profile and answers 100+ questions.)

You live more than an hour drive from me.

You are a smoker; cigarettes, cigars, 420, and/or vaping. (I'm highly sensitive to smoke.)

You are a drug user.

You are a convicted felon.

You do not have a valid driver's license.

You do not have a car.

You do have a car, but it's not operational.

You do not have a picture of your face on your profile.

You have a picture of your face on your profile, but it's blurry, not taken within the last year, from a distance and/or you're wearing sunglasses.

You have not written anything about yourself in your profile description.

You are jealous and/or possessive.

You have kids and they live with you full-time or most of the time.

Your profile contains negativity (i.e. no drama, gold diggers, fake women, everyone on here is a liar, etc.).

Clearly, I'm a picky, picky bitch.

HE: I'll be in St Pete tomorrow. Let's get together.

ME: I've already made plans for tomorrow night.

HE: How about Saturday?

ME: I've already made plans for Saturday.

HE: Sunday?

ME: Plans.

HE: You said you wanted to meet me. When are you free?

ME: I do want to meet you, but unfortunately, it's going to be 4 weeks out. I'm booked.

HE: WTF? It doesn't make sense that you're booked for over a month.

ME: If you actually read my profile, you would have recalled the first line that said, "I'm taking a break." You may also want to review that I'm a nationally touring comedian. I travel a lot. I booked this gig 8 months ago, and I got your email at 8:30 this morning.

HE: But if you really wanted to meet me, you'd make time for me.

ME: Not only am I going to be out of town, but I don't do whiny, pushy, needy, insecure, high maintenance, or passive aggressive.

HE: I read your profile. I'm not whining! I'm not passive aggressive. Fine! I'll leave you alone. I just thought we had something good together.

ME: We've never met! Oh, fuck this. (And... block.)

HE: Happy Sunday

ME: Happy Sunday to you too!

HE: I want to talk with you,. Its sunday . Will you come over and watch Movies with me.

ME: We can meet for coffee/lunch/dinner sometime next week and see if we click... but going to your place without meeting first is out of the question.

HE: I not asking ,.Im telling you what i want,.You can go play coffee date with some beta male. My way or forget it,.I dont take any crap from women,.

ME: And I don't take any crap from men.

(BLOCK)

HE: I'm ready to get off of this dating site. We should talk.

ME: (reads his profile)

HE: (seconds later) We should talk NOW

ME: (sigh) After reading your profile, I really don't think we're compatible. I'm not into dominant men.

HE: I see that someone other than me has said what you say they have said about my profile. Do you know the name of the person who has said this? Do you know who is doing the judging of me based on this profile? If I read off what that person says about your profile, I am absolutely certain that your personality and inclinations do not match the evaluator's assessment. BTW, I know a lot about hypnotism. Let me know if you ever want a sounding board regarding what you do.

ME: You judged you, not me. In your profile, it says "I'm really good at being a naturally dominant man." Look under the "Things I'm Really Good At" section in your profile. It's right next to where you forgot to mention you're an asshole. (and... BLOCK)

HE: (from a decent looking guy) I saw you looked at my profile and you didn't write me. I guess you want anything to do with an ugly guy like me.

ME: If you read MY profile, you would have seen I'm taking the month off. But thank goodness you wrote me first! Because now I know you have passive aggressive tendencies and have tremendous drama potential. I'll do us both a favor and just block you.

HE: Hi, I did read your profile to the end in all of it's entirety , I came out with one and only single conclusion ! that : There is no F***en way you are a funny girl in any way or shape ?or have any sense of humor? I guarantee it .. you might think you are ? or just wishing that you wannabe ?!! lol in your war declaration on men AKA" your profile " you took all and any shred of fun in the dating definition completely !!..lol I was going to say may be but now I am sure that you do not need a date or a man in your life ,? you need a puppet on strings like Dunham 's to move it any way and make it say what ever you please?! I am utterly shocked and so surprised that you are getting any responses at all from guys to who wants go out with you ??!!lol the must be a bunch of deranged guys who only looking only for sex but hide it when they are seeking it from a twisted and sickly infected state of mind woman who thinks that most men are a bunch of idiots who are dying to adore her strange personality for being supposedly different ?lol sorry ... .a retard !! lol oh my Lord .. I am going to run as fast as I could away from you , so I wouldn't get infected by your twisted sense of logic in choosing men which supposedly it is for normal men ?finally I say GOOD LUCK ... becaus eyou gonna need it so much ..lol

ME: Dear cl**ASS**ic p**ASS**ion, There's a BLOCK feature in this software. You should use it on people who don't interest you, like me! If you're not into strong women, why don't you skip online dating and look into mail-order brides from impoverished nations, Boku Haram kidnapping survivors, and if all else fails...there's always women in a coma.

Best of luck in your search!

ONLINE DATING FUN #8

Trivial trivia on online dating. Thank you, world wide web for the abundance of comedy material we never knew we needed!

"Desperate" daters are typically always available, are clingy, need constant relationship status updates, fish for compliments, drop their standards, and rationalize bad treatment.

Traci says: Okay... Newsflash! I'm still single!!! I'm not saying I'm desperate, but just wanted to let you know I've considered volunteering at a homeless shelter because all of those guys think I'm really pretty for a girl that doesn't do crank.

Six types of women that men tend to avoid are serial flirters, someone who talks about marriage too soon, clingy women, the party-girl, and a woman who talks too much or is a drama queen.

Traci says: So... cutie pie, sweetie, schnookie love muffin... we've known each other, I don't know, like 143 pages now, and I think it's time we have "the talk." You know "the talk" where I insist we at least get engaged and married in a month or two, because I know you have your shit together and I need to latch on to the goods while I can, and then I don't tell you I'm thinking about going off birth control so I can get knocked up and trap you in an endless Hell of "where's my money" and "it's your turn to watch Junior" while I go partying and picking arm wrestling fights with butch lesbians at Home Depot only to get arrested so I call you up at 3am asking you to bail me out of jail because I have unresolved "daddy" issues.

Four common date blunders include showing up late, talking about yourself too much, revealing too much about your ex, and an obvious over-eagerness.

Traci says: Sorry you were early, I couldn't get off the phone with my ex for 2 hours. I was telling him how amazing we are together, and that we're going to get married once we get past that court date from that alligator-wrestling incident...

Studies show that before a man even speaks a word, the way he stands (whether he is slouching or not) counts for over 80% of a woman's first impression.

Traci says: Just say NO to bad posture. Of course if a man meets a woman lying down, he's 80% sure he's going to screw her Domino's style... 30 minutes or less!

Studies show that men are put off by groups of loud women. If a woman wants to get a date, she should break away from a loud group to give a man a chance to approach her.

TRACI SCREAMS: I CAN'T REALLY MIMIC LOUD NOISES WHILE I'M TYPING OR WHILE YOU'RE READING THIS, SO YOU'LL JUST HAVE TO IMAGINE THAT I'M SCREAMING WHILE I'M TYPING IN ALL CAPS. OOOO... IT LOOKS LIKE YOU WANT TO MEET ME! LET ME EXCUSE MYSELF AND GO TO SOMEPLACE QUIETER. (Heads outside.) (Waits patiently for you to approach me now that it's quiet.) (Waits another 10 minutes, just in case you didn't realize I'm waiting for you to meet me.) (Waits another 10 minutes, just in case you didn't realize that I'm still waiting to meet you.) (Goes inside.) I DON'T KNOW WHAT THE HELL HIS PROBLEM IS...

Bad breath and bad teeth are an instant turn-off for potential dates. If deep dental cleaning doesn't improve a person's breath, he or she could have a stomach bacterium called *H. pylori*, which causes bad breath.

Traci says: I have found a direct correlation that if someone doesn't want to pay $12 a month for an online dating upgrade, $100 for a bi-annual dental cleaning is probably not going to happen either.

A man's top dating fears include that a woman will come between him and his friends, won't allow him free time, will turn out to be a stalker, won't respect him, or will be too high maintenance.

Traci says: That's bullshit. Women have those fears too. They just don't figure it out until it's way too late.

Signs that a woman is not interested in her date include avoiding eye contact, faking a smile or not smiling, leaning away, answering in monosyllables, sagging her shoulders, looking at her watch, tapping her foot, or staring blankly.

Traci says: Coincidentally, these are also signs of a stroke. If you see these signs, but the woman can still raise her hands above her head, you're not getting laid.

Signs that a man is about to break up with a woman include that he spends less time with her, he is no longer romantic, passionate kissing turns into quick pecks (particularly no kissing during sex), he fantasizes about someone else during sex, he pats her during a hug, and he tries to start fights.

Traci says: Yeah, we know.

Approximately 48% of online daters reported that their breakups occurred via email.

Traci says: I wonder what percentage of breakups occurred via sheriff's deputy?

In the online dating world, women are afraid of meeting a serial killer. Men are afraid of meeting someone "fat."

Traci says: This is crazy. I'm mostly afraid of meeting an overweight hermaphrodite serial killer.

According to Ann Rule (a true crime author, not a true statistician), about 3% of men are psychopaths, of which only a tiny percentage are serial killers.

Traci says: So, if I've had 97 dates where I didn't meet a psychopath, that means my next 3 dates could be very interesting...

In a survey of 5,000 singles conducted by Match.com, 43% said fresh breath mattered the most before a date, 17% said stylish clothes, 15% said sexy fragrance, 14% said good skin, and 10% said great hair.

Traci says: Fresh breath matters the most? Where is "not being a fucktard" on this list?

Nearly 40% of men do not feel confident meeting a woman for the first time.

Traci says: 100% of guys who don't show for a first date do not feel confident meeting a woman for the first time either.

Research has confirmed that women are more attracted to men who wear pheromone-based colognes or aftershaves such as 10X. Studies have also shown that women, who have a stronger sense of smell than men, are particularly attracted to musk and black licorice smells.

Traci says: My research has shown that 100% of my dates end up with a blow job if they show up wearing Stetson Cologne, carrying a box of Belgian chocolates, and a bottle of Ouzo... okay that's never happened. They never show up with Ouzo.

Top 10 turn-offs for women include cystic acne, raggedy nails, flatulence and belching, missing teeth, body odor, bad breath, hairy nostrils, "man boobs," "goofy" glasses, and hair "mistakes."

Traci says: Other turn-offs include canceling the date while I'm on my way to the date, not showing up for the date, and slipping me a roofie.

WHY THE FUCK
DID YOU WRITE ME?

"If you can't say nothing nice, don't say nothing at all." ~Thumper from Bambi

I can't imagine why these guys looked at my pics and/or read my profile and felt like they needed to say something negative to me, but they did. This book is proof that I am not everyone's ideal girlfriend. And if I'm not your type, you owe it to yourself to leave me the fuck alone. Block me. Hide me. You don't need my approval. You've actually done both of us a favor by blocking me. But no... it's not that easy.

Some pathetic troll sees a relatively happy woman on the internet and needs to tell her that she's not for him, because in some small way it makes him feel better about himself. Yes... it's important to let this woman know that not every man in the online dating world wants her.

In all of these cases, my responses were what I wanted to write, but never sent. No sense aggravating the trolls. But clearly, I am "Dim Sum" for weirdos.

HE: To bad you're in Florida cause I'm looking for someone who lives in Cleveland Ohio area..Well good luck in your search

ME: The loss is obviously mine. To think, I've chosen a life in warm, sunny Florida with its stupid sandy beaches and beautiful gulf views... over a life with you in Cleveland, OH, with its unpredictable cloudy weather, cold rain, and lake-effect snow. What's wrong with me?

HE: sorry cats are a deal breaker

ME: I totally get why you had to tell me you rejected me, especially since I never expressed interest in you in the first place. I want to ensure my chances of never meeting you, so I'm adopting 7 more cats! Meow and Ciao!

HE: Hi! I don't think we are a match in the slightest but would love to have a drink and chat with you as your profile was wonderful to read.

ME: I'm glad you enjoyed my profile! Unfortunately, I'm so busy meeting all the other people I'm incompatible with, I just don't have time to meet you, too. It's a shame that meeting incompatible people is not only such a waste of time, but a great way to remain single as well! I can't believe more people don't do this.

HE: You're almost perfect! But you're not 420 friendly.

ME: Per my profile... I'm allergic to smoke. I'm also allergic to Taco Bell, Doritos, and people who can't remember shit.

HE: Hi! It's "Paul." We were going to meet a few months back. How are you

ME: How am I? How are you? You cancelled our Scrabble date 4 months ago because you got the flu... nanoseconds before we were supposed to meet. Must've been some flu if it rendered you incapable of communication, for 4 months. YUO OLNY GTE OEN CCHANE OT MKAE A FRIST IMERPSISON ADN YUO BELW TI.

HE: Figured I'd say hello since you were my highest match. 92%

ME: Your profile contains one blurry picture and no description. Near as I can tell, the 92% we have in common is dark hair, an ugly sweater, and a mustache.

HE: Hi there. I'd like to talk to you.

HIS PROFILE (and this is ALL that it says): Not a big drinker. Never been arrested.

ME: Why haven't you been arrested?

ONLINE DATING FUN #9

Seventeen more things you should never say on a first date... unless you need to end it fast and faking your death isn't an option.

Not going to lie... I've said most of these.

- Your man-boobs look just like my mom's. She had the best man-boobs.

- Congratulations! You're the first person in 2 years I haven't slept with on the first date.

- Did you bring your STD results with you?

- Text me first, please don't call me. My spouse doesn't know I'm dating yet.

- You're a little smaller than I'm used to... yes. Of course I was talking about your penis.

- OMG – that ass is just perfect!!! Please tell me you're into anal. Receiving.

- You're really nice, but from your pics I thought you were a trannie.

- Let me get this straight... you met someone on Craigslist last week, dressed in drag, and you're surprised they beat the shit out of you? (True story)

- Have you ever had any wild fantasies about getting your ass kicked by a Dominatrix? Oops... must've confused you with someone else. Check, please!

- Never have I ever... had an interracial gang bang. Hey... where are you going? That stupid game was your idea!

- I found this really cool restaurant on Groupon...

- My ex just won't leave me alone. I try to tell her I'm over her, but she doesn't believe it.

- Change in dinner plans... I got fired today.

- You are WAY better than the guy I had coffee with earlier today.

- I'm not looking for anything serious.

- I think we'll make great friends.

- Let's just skip all this and go back to my place.

EMAILS THAT WORKED

(Just kidding!)

EMAILS THAT WORKED

I wish I had more of these to offer you, but here are some emails I received that I responded to, with explanations as to why I responded to them. Keep in mind, I'm looking for educated guys with a sense of humor. Personal details have been changed to protect identities.

My profile at the time I received this inquiry kicked off with "Please read my profile. I'm probably not the droid you're looking for," which the writer refers to.

#1

HE: It may be hard to believe but, after carefully reading your profile, you just might be the droid I'm looking for. I like that your filter doesn't work well. Mine doesn't, either... if I still have it. I may have lost it along the way.

In terms of music, jazz fusion, rap, and EMD are in the list of what I don't like. Almost anything else works. I like live music and I like swing dancing.

I never progressed to being able to play piano and sing at the same time. I can play blues harp and sing, but it's not quite the same. I've never tried singing while playing my "xylophone." I think it would be safe to say you're likely a much better singer than me :) What kind of music do you perform?

I'm divorced and have two children, ages 26 and 28. I have less than no desire to have any more children so I went to the doctor and made sure it can't happen.

By the way, I like the *Alice in Wonderland* and *Star Wars* references... and Waffle House is the bomb, with the best hash browns (scattered, smothered, and covered, please) around!

I'm not easily offended. I'm sure I can be offended but it would take a lot, so I'll be happy to have a seat and get the first round.

This was supposed to be a short note but it didn't turn out that way. Sorry about that. "Larry"

WHY I RESPONDED

"Larry" took the time to write a beautifully personalized note, referring to specific points in my profile that spoke to him while elaborating on things that were not necessarily detailed in his profile. His response was polite, respectful, and I just got the feeling he was a really nice guy. I wrote "Larry" back, and we met for dinner the following week. I really enjoyed my 3-4 weeks dating "Larry." I learned the basics of the style of swing dancing he enjoyed, and he enjoyed my drive-by hypnosis sessions. Unfortunately, "Larry" and I both had some family issues that required immediate attention, and we ended up going our separate ways.

#2

HE: Okay, so you are my top match and I absolutely love that. I read through all of our likes and dislikes and it seems as though we have definitely got to meet each other. My name is "Jay" I'm a retired professional musician now working in home renovation for the time being and I have an art company it is kind of on the back burner right now. I love the fact that you're a stand-up comic and a musical one at that and the tattoo on your back is absolutely amazing, plus you're pretty damn good looking LOL. I love a girl in a corset. Hope to hear back from you. Until then have a great day and weekend

WHY I RESPONDED

"Jay" wrote a really nice personalized note, and he acknowledged that we were a good match. He took the time to read through and compare our likes and dislikes. This shows me he's truly interested in finding a compatible partner. I received this inquiry a few weeks before a vacation and we have not met yet, but I'm sure we will in the next few weeks.

#3

HE: Loved your profile, really spoke to me. I also travel for work , mostly between Tampa and the West Coast. I'm in Tampa quite often. The work you are doing sounds very cool . I'm curious to know more .....;) My work is also involves holistic healing as well. "Jerry"

WHY I RESPONDED

You can't tell much from his initial email, but when I went back and read his profile I discovered "Jerry" was a truly fascinating person. Even if he wasn't for me as a life partner because he travels so much. I definitely wanted to meet him, as you can tell by how I responded...

ME: Your profile was funny as hell! 80's comedy collection, cuddler, ethical warrior, and needing a muse spoke to me. :) I'd love to share coffee/lunch/dinner when you're in town and learn more how an ex-Ninja baker turned holistic healer came to be. Please give me as much notice as you can as I'm often booked for comedy gigs. Cheers my new friend, Traci

"Jerry" and I dated when he was in town over 2-3 months. He had a beautiful energy, a passion for what he does, and one of the best senses of humor I've ever come across in a non-comedian. I stopped dating "Jerry" when I began dating another man who lived closer and was much more available. "Jerry" and I still remain good friends.

#4

At the time I received this email from "Eugene," I had posted several of the goofier emails I received, including: "Do you like young guys with big fat cocks?" Eugene kicked off his inquiry with my punchline.

HE: "Honestly, I like old guys with big fat wallets a lot more. An oxygen tank and IV painkillers being carried in to the bedroom by a Hospice employee is enough to make me orgasm."

I just blew coffee everywhere! Thanks!!

WHY I RESPONDED

"Eugene" showed me he liked my sense of humor right away. Similar to "Jerry," "Eugene" had a fascinating profile and I really wanted to get to know him even though I knew he lived elsewhere and was just "passing through." He has a PhD and works in medicine, but also has a passion for racing. He definitely likes to live life to the fullest, as I do too.

"Eugene" and I met 2 years ago. He travels a lot for work, but we still get together when our schedules allow, which is about 2 or 3x a year. Our conversations are always spirited and we enjoy catching up on each other's travels. We still remain good friends.

#5

HE: Although I don't have "Meet Me" option, I saw that you did click "Meet Me" and thought I would seek you out and see what's up. I dug through all the profiles within the surrounding area and finally found yours. Pretty impressive and straight to the point – unlike most I've seen on this site. I think I fit most of what you state except for "the lifestyle" or bdsm which I've never been exposed but certainly open to. I like to travel also but these days I'm a contractor on a large software project that involves my nights and weekends at the moment which may put a damper on things. You are very pretty and I wanted to reach out to you anyway!

WHY I RESPONDED

This guy is a free member, and admitted he had to dig around the website to find me after he saw I liked him. He acknowledged my profile was different than "my competition," and admitted he didn't know much about "the lifestyle" but was open it. He took the time to read my profile, he was respectful, his pictures were nice, and he wrote a personalized response. We met for coffee, and there is some interest so we will probably meet again when our work schedules allow.

To conclude this chapter, I think it's fair to say that I generally will respond to an online dating inquiry under the following conditions:

- the sender has the appearance of someone who could fit into my world.

- the email to me was personalized.

- the sender showed an interest in getting to know me.

- the sender had the appearance of being friendly and respectful.

- the sender demonstrated he has interesting hobbies and/or an interesting profession.

I will elaborate on these and more in the next chapter.

TRACI'S PROFILE TIPS

"You attract what you are, not what you want.
If you want great, you have to be great."
~Unknown

Obviously, I'm not a professional dating researcher. I'm a single person trying to find another single person who shares the same values, dreams, and beliefs that I do. What I'm sharing with you are the things that make me swipe right (yes!), and the things that make me swipe left (Hell no!). This isn't based on science, this is based on my personal preferences and experience after reviewing thousands of profiles and emails. In my mind, each profile is made up of pieces, like a puzzle. If the pieces I see indicate a pleasing picture, I find myself wanting to know more about that person. If the pieces I see make an ugly picture or are incomplete, I simply move on. With millions of people in the online dating pools... finding someone compatible is simply a numbers game.

Some people just need to play the game longer because their current situation is loaded with personal challenges. Be patient, keep your sense of humor, don't take anything personal, and don't lose faith. With any luck, these tips will help you weed out the riff raff, so you can spend your time meeting the best people for you.

Your Profile Name

I recommend a profile name that is easy to remember, positive, and says something about yourself.

BeachLover123

GuyFromFLandOH

WhiteKnight

AnimalLuvr

FunnyChick

YogaLuver

I personally avoid profile names that smack of negativity. If I see names like these, I automatically disqualify them. They are not serious about meeting someone, or seriously jaded.

TryinThisAgain

HopelessGuy4U

Slutty1-4U

RUReal

LetsFukSoon

LikMyBalz

Your Profile Pictures

We are a visual-based society. People often underestimate the importance of good profile pictures. The bottom line of online dating is all about "selling yourself" to another person. If you've read a few online dating profiles, you know that most people have NO idea how to do this. We can sell our stuff online, no problem. If you're selling a car online, you simply take pictures of that car from every angle, and post it. Done. When it comes to putting pictures of ourselves online? Uh-oh. Now we have to confront all the things about us we don't like, and we sure as heck don't want to put them online for the whole world to see! We don't want to admit we are too fat, too skinny, too short, too tall, or too ugly.

Whether your body is a moped or a luxury SUV, here are a few tips on how to photograph yourself, and what photographs to show in order to make the best impression possible.

HYGIENE

Before you take a picture of yourself, wash, groom, shave, wax, trim, hair cut, make-up, etc so you're shiny! I can't tell you how many photos from guys I've seen where they look like they've been woken up seconds before and dragged through a wife beater t-shirt blender. Women – just wear make-up that enhances your best features, but still looks natural.

SMILE!

Your profile should include at least one headshot of you smiling. I say this, because I look for happy people to date. I don't want to date some nasty frowny-faced curmudgeon. If you can't muster up one picture of you enjoying life, then I'm pretty sure I don't want to be with you.

FULL BODY

Your profile should include at least one picture of your entire body, clothed. Wear something clean, nice, wrinkle free, and casual. Back to the car analogy... no one buys a car with just a picture of the door, roof, or tail light. They want to see the whole car. People are no different. You don't need to show off every angle, but the person looking at you wants some idea of your height vs weight. Speaking of weight...

weight for it...

weight for it...

WEIGHT HATE

The person who is considering asking you on a date wants to know what you look like NOW. If you have a few extra pounds, own every single one of them. If you're not happy with yourself, then while you're single is a great time to get off your ass and do something about it. Post a full body pic of you. Some people will love you and all your love handle glory, and some people will not enjoy your extra cushion for the pushin'. Not everyone is going to like you, and not everyone has to like you. In online dating, it's critical that you be true to yourself and honest with others who might be considering you for a relationship.

A NOTE ABOUT WEIGHT HATE

Before anyone goes off on me about my "own your shit" attitude on weight... I'll tell you right now I've been an overweight woman for most of my adult life, weighing close to 250 pounds at one time. I know all too well the discrimination and pressures of not having a Playboy Bunny figure. My lifetime of yo-yo dieting, and how I lost 91 pounds only to put 50 of them back on during my divorce and taking care of my mother is for another book. If you are overweight, you owe it to yourself to 1) educate yourself on how to eat healthy, 2) figure out why you don't eat healthy, and 3) start exercising and get healthy.

The internet is loaded with great tips on eating healthy. Hypnosis and hypnotherapy are great, surprisingly cost-effective ways to find your triggers and fix them. In the meantime, forgive yourself for being fat. Thank those extra pounds for protecting you, and release them from service. It's time to love yourself and commit to making yourself the best person you can be.

I've conquered many of my food challenges with hypnotherapy including a wicked cookie addiction, and I use hypnosis to motivate me to exercise and to lift heavier weights. I began meeting with a personal trainer 18 months ago at this writing. I've only lost 5 pounds, but I'm down 2 clothing sizes and physically the strongest I've ever been. I feel great, my confidence is much higher, and I'm proud of the commitment I've made to becoming the next best version of myself.

TIME TRAVELERS

Make sure your picture is current. Do not post pics of you that are older than 2 years. Pics that show a photo chronology of the person from a cute little child in the 70s to the fat, balding old fart you were 5 years ago shows that someone is not comfortable with their present-day self. No one is dating "15 years ago YOU." They're dating you NOW. Do us all a favor, and be whoever you are now.

BEARDS

One of my pet peeves, is men who post pics of them clean shaven, with 5 o'clock shadow, with 5-hour stubble, 5-day scrub, various goatees, and with a full blown Amish beard. Which one am I going to get? If you're going to do that, then at least post a caption with one that says: "What I look like now." I can't tell you how many dates I've gone on looking for Mr. Clean, and then "Grizzly Adams" shows up. "Oh! I didn't recognize you..." is not a good way to start a first date.

QUALITY, NOT QUANTITY

A picture may say 1000 words, but 1000 pictures say you're desperate! Post no more than 4-8 pictures. Anyone who maximizes their photo quota can appear they're bragging and/or insecure to others. Face pic, body pic, and other pics of you having fun or visiting cool places will give the person a good feel for what you're about.

KEEP FRIENDS AND FAMILY OUT OF IT

Avoid posting pics of you with your friends or family, unless you crop them out or hide their faces. In my opinion, posting pics without permission of those you are closest to shows a total lack of respect for their privacy... not to mention the person looking at your profile has no idea which one is YOU. When I see a guy posting photos of him with his buddies, I get the feeling I know where his priorities are, and I'm not going to be one of them. If you do post a picture of you with someone of the opposite sex, identify who the other person is. Don't leave us guessing if that person is your wife, sister, daughter, or ex-girlfriend.

I WEAR MY SUNGLASSES AT NIGHT

As a rule, I do not engage with profiles where the person has 5 pics, and he/she's wearing sunglasses in all of them. The eyes are the windows to the soul. If you don't have eyes, you don't have a soul, and more often than not that person is cheating on his/her partner.

BLURRY PICS

With camera phones being so good nowadays, I'm amazed at how many pics are blurry. Seriously? Usually, when I come across a profile with blurry pics, the pics are typically older, and there's a damn good reason why the profile owner has a blurry pic. In my experience, the person hasn't aged well, isn't technology savvy, and/or has something to hide. Disqualified!

OTHER PICTURES

If the profile owner doesn't show a picture of him/herself, again... there's a reason. Often times, the person is looking to cheat, cheating on a spouse, or is insecure in his looks and feels his cute puppies or penis-extension car is more likely to get him attention. When you call them on it, they say, "I can't show my face because of work." BULLSHIT. 99% of the time, they're cheating on their significant other or spying on a spouse/co-worker.

PICTURES I LIKE

I like pictures that show a person's sense of humor, cool places they've gone, hobbies, sporting events and pets. It shows they already have a life and what's important to them. Having pics that show who you are is important, especially if you're not much of a writer. When you post pics, keep in the back of your mind "What kind of person would be impressed by these photos?" I love when I see a photo from a guy who posts picture of him with his Lamborghini (or other high-end sports car), and then he writes in the profile "No gold diggin' hos." Uh huh.

Your Profile Description

I'm repeating myself, but it's so important: Be honest about who and what you are. I'm still befuddled when someone 30+ years has no clue how to describe themselves or what they're interested in. In my experience, when a person can't take the time to describe themselves, they're either lazy, not serious about finding someone, truly have no life to speak of, or really busy. I click through these profiles, because I don't want to date any guy who doesn't know who he is, or is too lazy to figure it out.

I encourage everyone to be YOU. Be REAL, be proud of who you are, and be proud of what you've done. If you're not proud of you, now's the time to make some changes in your life! If you don't know how to begin describing yourself, ask your friends how they would describe you. Then start your profile with "My friends will tell you I'm _____, _____, and _____." You can't get more honest than that. And if your friends say you're an asshole... now's the time to own your asshole-ness, or start making changes for the better.

HOBBIES and INTERESTS

Next up – What are your hobbies? If you find this hard to answer, ask yourself, "What the heck do I do in my spare time?" There's your answer.

Before I started dating, I had no idea how many men love fishing, camping, and the great outdoors. I am not outdoorsy at all. I go outside for 2 reasons: that's where my car is parked, and that's where my hot tub is. My policy is no A/C, no Traci. As for camping, I'm part Arab. It took my family thousands of years to get out of a tent, I'm not going back in. I'm sure there are several women out there who love the outdoors but I am not one of them. By taking a few minutes to list your interests in your profile, you increase your chances of finding people who dig the same things as you, and you're not wasting time on the people who don't.

YOUR FAMILY

Do you have kids, parents, or other family members you're responsible for? How about pets?

Don't be afraid to say how many dependents you're responsible for, give their ages, and detail your custody situation. Family comes first, and your potential partner has a right to know if they're coming in 2nd or 22nd place in your heart.

BE SPECIFIC

Above all, be thorough about who you are and what you're looking for. Someone out there is looking for someone JUST LIKE YOU. If they're not looking for someone just like you, I'll bet they're willing to settle for someone close enough. But if you don't detail who that is and stand out from the rest of millions of singles out there, you'll never find the gate keeper to your key master. If you're looking for someone to raise your 6 year old, say so. Somewhere out there, there's a SuperMom or SuperDad who would be more than willing to help raise your child. If you don't want children or can't have children, say that! If you only like tall women, bald men, physically fit people – say that! Yes, being specific will make your eligible dating pool smaller, but on the other hand? You're more likely to find the imperfectly right person for you.

LET'S TALK ABOUT SEX

If you're looking for NSA sex (no strings attached), say so, keeping in mind the guidelines of the website you're searching on. Don't be afraid to be specific... especially if you're into freakier things. I guarantee you someone else out there is looking for the same things as you. I do get weirded out when these sex requests come from Facebook friends or vanilla dating sites, versus sites that are specifically designed for sexual encounters. Which brings me to the next sex-tion...

LOOKING FOR LOVE IN ALL THE WRONG PLACES

So many people aren't looking for love in all the right places. What's the most important thing for you? Are you looking for a life partner, or a partner for 1 night? I'm not being critical of either, but maybe specifying your search will bring you the results you're looking for. What is most important to you? Religion? Politics? Sports? I guarantee you there's a dating site that caters specifically to your religion, your politics, or your sport. You might also try MeetUp.com to see what groups are out there for more casual settings. If there isn't a MeetUp group, go ahead and make one up! What have you got to lose?

If you're looking for a partner for 1 night, then perhaps you should look into sites that cater towards sexual encounters. There are several good ones, and sometimes they're just as reasonably priced as the more conventional dating sites. The point of this whole section is, it's time to think outside the big dating box. Decide on what you want, and then research who else had the same idea as you.

TRACI'S DATING TIPS

To write a book about all the responses I got, without sharing some of the things I've learned in online dating would be pretty irresponsible. So here are a few tips I found to be helpful, and with any luck they'll soften the bumps as you toss and tumble through your online dating journey.

If It Isn't Fun, It's Not Worth Doing

This is my overall philosophy in everything I do. Same with online dating! If it isn't fun, then it's not worth doing. So many people take dating so seriously and get bent out of shape as if every person they bumped into online was there just to ruin their life. I get it. You are, in theory, meeting someone who could potentially be your soulmate and make the rest of your life an amazing journey, or you could meet the succubus who will break you and take you for all you're worth. But so many people put emphasis on the destination of finding their soulmate, that they forget to enrich their personal lives until their soulmate comes along, as well as not enjoying other people they meet along the way.

If you're currently single, now is the time to explore and learn. Go back to school. Take classes and learn things that interest you. Find groups of people with the same hobbies as you. There's no reason why you have to stop living and learning, simply because you don't have a soulmate. Work on becoming the next best version of yourself, whatever that next best version may be.

Be Interesting

I will give one of my hypnosis instructors, Mark Cunningham, Renegade Hypnotist Extraordinaire, the credit for this one. People are instantly attracted to people who have done things and been places. They have lived. They have experienced things most people will never do or have the guts to try. They are interesting. One gentleman contacted me because he thought being a comedian was fascinating. I wrote him back because he loved racing cars. Another gentleman contacted me because he's always been fascinated with hypnosis. I wrote him back because he was an artist that specialized in plaster casts of bodies. If there's something on your bucket list... don't wait until you have your soulmate to check it off. Live NOW.

Be Honest

"Traci, you've said this a hundred times already," but I mean it! Don't lie in your profile. Be your age. Be your height. Be your weight. Be a geek. Be neurotic. Be proud of who you are, and be honest about what you're looking for. If you're looking to have 6 kids in the next 3 years, say so! If you only want a booty call for tonight, say so! When you lie, it highlights what you don't like about yourself. It shows you're ashamed of being you and/or you have something to hide. Don't worry about what others think. Focus on being the person that is you, and focus on finding the people that want someone like you. If you're ashamed to be you and you know you have things you need to fix, now's a great time to start working on the next best version of yourself. Are you getting the point I'm trying to make yet?

Be Specific

Every now and then, I get someone who says, "Wow, your profile is long! I'm not gonna read all that shit." My profile is long for a reason. I know exactly what kind of person I am looking for. I don't know what he's going to look like, but I know the attitude and beliefs all too well because I want my partner to share those with me. Those viewing my profile know what they are looking for. If the person viewing my pics doesn't want to take the time to read my profile, then we are both looking for different things and that's okay. If someone doesn't want to take a few minutes to get to know me, doesn't like how I spend my spare time, doesn't agree with my politics, or doesn't like that I have 2 cats... that's OKAY. I only want to meet those people who are best suited for me. Yes, it has occurred to me that I'm too off-the-wall and no one out there is suited for me! I'm okay with that, too.

A Word About Attraction

Attraction is just one step in the dating process. Not much happens unless there is attraction. When screening for people for long-term relationships, there is the thought, "How will this person fit into my world?" If the sender wrote me first and took time to write the note he did, he obviously felt there was a chance I would fit into his world just fine. Of course, you never know until you actually meet each other. If I get the general impression this person will fit into my world, I am more inclined to write back.

"Looks" and "Appearances" are literally the ugliest part of dating. There are lots of sweet, amazing people who are not gifted with jaw-dropping genetics. There are a lot of "beautiful people" who are not gifted with manners and etiquette. Read the profile and the emails very carefully. If it's overflowing with negativity and expectations... you can pretty much tell your "white knight" has a few chinks in his armor, or your "Princess" is a Royal Hine-Ass.

Freaks Attract Freaks

Whatever you are right now is (most likely) what you're going to attract. Fit people attract fit people. Smart people attract smart people. Pretty people attract pretty people. Heavy people attract heavy people. Stupid people attract stupid people. Freaks attract freaks. If you don't like what you're attracting, then while you're single is the best time to work on becoming the person you've always wanted to be. Constant bitching why rich people don't want to date your broke ass, or why fitness models don't want to date your fat ass... changes nothing. It's one of those harsh realities of life. If you're not happy with you, your only choices are to accept you, or change you.

Don't Be Afraid of the Bad Dates

In comedy, I learned more about myself as a person and as a comedian when I had a crappy show, than when the show was amazing. Same with dating! I learned more about myself and what I didn't want when I met someone who wasn't right for me.

I dated one gentleman who was a 99% match according to OKCupid. At first he seemed perfect as we got along on so many levels... until I realized he had no control over his work schedule, and very little respect for mine. He'd get called in to work on the way to our date, canceling on the way to see me, and then try and reschedule me over appointments I had booked weeks in advance. I discovered I have no tolerance for constant last-minute cancelations... and the 99% we had in common became a big ZERO. Time to re-adjust my search criteria to someone who has control over their work schedule.

Energy Doesn't Lie

The one thing online dating does best... is prevent the energy between two beings to interact. I can read everything about a person. I can perv their pics 100 times. But until I'm in the presence of that person? I have no idea if we're going to connect or not. I've had some fiery connections online, only to meet the individual in person and wonder what I missed, because he wasn't the person I thought he was. Other times, I'm pretty nonchalant about meeting someone, and then the sparks fly! Sometimes the first few dates were okay, but it wasn't until date 3 or 4 that the "WOW!" factor kicked in.

The point of all this, is **energy doesn't lie.**

If it feels good, follow it a little further. If it feels wrong, don't follow it anymore. Trust your instincts.

NO DRAMA

One of my pet peeves, is that every other profile I read says "No drama."

Okay... who openly admits they are drama? That's right... NO ONE admits they are drama! You want to avoid drama? Stop dating HUMANS. It's the only way. Putting "NO DRAMA" on your profile doesn't do shit to keep drama away. All it does is put people on notice that you're looking for it. Put what you DO want in a partner on your profile. You're more likely to attract it and find it.

Don't Settle

We all have things that we want in a partner, and we all have things we've experienced in others that piss us off to no end. It's important to clearly identify what these are. I'm completely emotionally driven, so I could follow a good energy with someone, yet they're wrong for me. So I have a back-up system, which I call: Traci's Rate-a-Date System.

The 10 things listed on the chart are important to me in a partner (not necessarily in order). Each of these I gave a score from 1-10. This system enables me to think realistically instead of emotionally about each date, and whether they are really what I'm looking for. In the table, the scores represent real guys I met and went out with, but the names have been changed. I had a nice connection with all of these men. But when it came down to what was important to me? The scores really showed who I should focus on.

For instance, I really liked "Donny." We had a LOT in common professionally. Unfortunately, he lost points for living in Canada, and his priority will be his 2 beautiful daughters, who are 12 and 15 (as it should be). I met "Freddy" a few weeks ago. He has no dependents, lives a few miles from my house, and he's a lot of fun... so I'll be putting a bit more effort into seeing where that goes.

You can customize the Rate-A-Date System to be as detailed or as vague as you like. Feel free to add other traits and values that you find important. I only kept things simple to illustrate how it works, and to show that I have anal-retentive tendencies.

Traci's Rate-a-Date System

Description	Criteria	Allen	Bubba	Cedric	Donny	Ethan	Freddy	George
FUN	10-Fun; 5-Moderately Fun; 1-Stick In The Mud	10	10	10	7	10	10	1
JOB	10-Retired; 7-Working A Job He Loves; 4-Working A Job He Doesn't Love; 1-Not Working	8	8	8	8	8	8	10
FINANCIAL INDEPENDENCE	10-Financially Independent; 5-Working Towards Financial Independence; 1-You're Going To Support This One	1	10	5	7	10	5	10
POLITICS	10-Agrees With Me; 5-We Agree On Some Things, Disagree On Others; 0-Disagrees With Me Completely	5	10	0	0	10	10	5
INTELLIGENCE/ CONVERSATION	10-Smart, Witty, Keeps Things Going But A Great Listening; 5-Looks To Me To Keep Things Going; 1-Boring, Overbearing, Doesn't Listen To Me	10	10	10	5	10	8	5
RELATIONSHIP BALANCE	10-Balanced; 5-More Submissive; 1-More Dominant	7	10	10	10	7	10	1
LIVES NEAR ME	10-St Pete; 8-Tampa; 5-Bradenton; 3-Orlando; 0-Anywhere Else	3	0	0	0	8	10	3
DEPENDENTS (Kids and/or parents to care for)	10-No Dependents; 8-Dependents Gone In 3 Years; 5-Dependents Gone in 5 Years; 1-Dependents 10+ Years	10	4	10	1	4	10	10
LOOKS	10-Adorable; 5-Okay; 1-Not So Much	10	5	8	10	10	10	8
BODY	10 - Fit; 5-Working On It; 1 Not so Much	1	5	9	6	7	10	5
TOTAL		65	72	70	54	84	91	58

TIPS ON HOW TO RESPOND TO A PROFILE

In my opinion, the best way to get someone to respond to your inquiry, is to only respond to someone who took the time to write a good profile, post pics reflecting who they are, and most importantly, someone you are truly interested in meeting.

Once you find a good profile with some details and pictures that are consistent, AND it resonates with you, then take a few minutes to write a personalized note highlighting 2 or 3 things in that profile that truly spoke to you. For instance, this is something I might write:

Hi (insert profile name), I'm Traci. Your profile really spoke to me, especially since you mentioned that your favorite author is Ayn Rand. *The Fountainhead* is my fav book of hers. I see you enjoy Scrabble as well. If my profile interests you, can I suggest we meet for a game of Scrabble? If not, I wish you all the best in your search. Thank you, Traci

If the person writes you back – great! If the person doesn't write you back, don't follow up with "Please write me back!" or "WTF, I saw you checking me out." Simply, wait for the response. They will either write you back, or they won't. Give them the benefit of the doubt. If you don't hear back in a month, write back again.

> Just dropping you another note in case my first one got lost in your inbox. I'm still interested in playing Scrabble.

If no answer... try again a month later. Perhaps the person is traveling, busy with work, found someone, whatever. If they don't answer after the third attempt, stop.

There is nothing worse than receiving a form letter. Your chances of getting a response will increase exponentially when you take a sincere interest in the person, show them what you have in common, and make a conscious effort to stand out from the pack. Let the person know you chose them, and here's why. You'll get more responses with personalized honey, than by peppering the world with "Hey."

Speaking of "Hey..."

HEY!

Thanks for reading my first endeavor in bathroom literature. I hope you liked it.

If you got more enjoyment out of this book than the $15 you put into it, I'm delighted.

If you didn't, then you're probably one of those people who bitches about everything you do, and that takes a lot more than $15 to fix.

If you have any questions or comments, don't hesitate to write me at www.HeyTraci.com. I'd love to hear about your dating stories, good or bad. Of course, I'd be more thrilled if one of you STILL wanted to date me after reading this shit... but I guess only time will tell.

Until then, I wish you all the best in your search for happiness... or unhappiness, as it may be.

There are only good times... and better stories.

The choice is ALWAYS yours.

With more love than I ever gave you on the acknowledgments page,
Traci

ABOUT THE AUTHOR

Traci Kanaan was born and raised in Berea, OH. She attended Berea High School, then Otterbein University graduating with a B.A. in Music and Business with minors in Music Composition, Piano Performance, and Electronic Music.

She moved to Palmetto, FL, in 1995 and started Traci Keychain Advertising Specialties, Inc, where she sold promotional products and corporate gifts to local businesses until she sold the accounts in 2014.

In 2002, Traci performed at her first open mic, and was bitten hard by the stand-up comedy bug. She eventually became known as The Princess of Parodies, and released her first (and only) comedy CD in 2009, called *Tinkle Tinkle Little Star*. Also in 2009, Traci was hired to perform at a clothing optional resort, and seeing an opportunity to expand her market, began creating another musical comedy show specifically for swingers, nudists, and BDSMers (those into bondage, discipline, and sado-masochism). Her comedy persona for that market is known as The Dominatrix of Ditties, and she was voted Top Female Entertainer by the Annual Lifestyle Awards in 2015, 2016, and 2017.

In addition to being a comedian, Traci is also a Certified Hypnotist, Certified Clinical Hypnotherapist, and Stage Hypnotist. She owns Wings Hypnosis, LLC, and very much enjoys helping her clients overcome whatever challenges are holding them back from the life they've always dreamed about living.

Traci currently resides in St. Petersburg, FL, where she is a therapy human for her 2 Siamese cats, Thelma and Louise.

Made in the USA
Columbia, SC
19 January 2018